SCIENCE
COMPUTER PROGRAMS
for kids and other people

Apple® Version

Tom Speitel, Ph.D.

Mike Rook

Khan Pannell

Cornelia Anguay

Danny Speitel

ILLUSTRATIONS BY KHAN PANNELL

SCIENCE
COMPUTER PROGRAMS
for kids and other people

Apple® Version

A RESTON COMPUTER GROUP BOOK
Reston Publishing Company, Inc.
A Prentice-Hall Company
Reston, Virginia

100406

Library of Congress Cataloging in Publication Data
Main entry under title:

Science computer programs for kids and other people.

"A Reston Computer Group book."
Includes index.
Summary: Programs, to be used on the Apple computer,
present concepts in various science fields, such as
astronomy, biology, and physics.
  1. Science—Computer programs—Juvenile literature.
2. Apple computer—Programming—Juvenile literature.
[1. Science—Computer programs. 2. Apple computer—
Programming] I. Speitel, Tom. II. Pannell, Khan, ill.
Q183.9.S28   1984   502.8'5425   84-2099
ISBN 0-8359-6901-0

Editorial/production supervision and interior design
by Barbara J. Gardetto

© 1984 by
Reston Publishing Company, Inc.
A Prentice-Hall Company
Reston, Virginia 22090

10   9   8   7   6   5   4   3   2   1

Printed in the United States of America

disclaimer

Reston Publishing Company and the authors will have no liability or responsibility to the purchaser or any other person or entity with respect to any liability, loss, or damage caused or alleged to be caused directly or indirectly by this book or its use, including but not limited to any interruption in service, loss of business, or consequential damages resulting from the use of this product.

The word Apple® is a registered trademark of Apple Computer Incorporated. Apple Computer Incorporated was not in any way involved in the writing or preparation of this book. Use of the term Apple should not be construed to represent any endorsement, official or otherwise, by Apple Computer Incorporated.

acknowledgments

Our greatest thanks go to our spouses, children, and friends who supported us with confidence during the writing and illustration of this book. Their names are Rita and Ian Speitel; Diane Rook; Terry Papen; Zac, Dan, and Gil Anguay; Marie Hawkins; John Hawkins; and Dr. Steve Coles.

The words of encouragement from staff of the University of Hawaii helped stimulate the writing during many months of labor. Thanks to Dr. Sanford Siegel, Dr. Barbara Siegel, Dr. E. Barbara Klemm, Dr. Chuck Guili, Dr. Frank Pottenger, Will Kyselka, Lee Kyselka, Dr. James Harpstrite, and Donald Young.

contents

to the kids

This book and your Apple will make science come alive. All of the programs in this book are fun. Most make pictures and do things. You can launch a satellite, dock a space module, race a sailboat, grow organisms, or make a stroboscope.

Start using this book by copying programs which look interesting to you. Choose the short ones, such as Constant Velocity, first. After you have a program running, try changing it a little. You control the computer. Make it work for you by using your own customized programs for your science projects.

If you run into trouble, ask your parents, teachers or friends for help.

to the adult—
parent or teacher

This book is designed for students in grades six through twelve. It is intended for self study but may also be used in classroom and science fair settings. APPLESOFT BASIC on disk systems is the vehicle for learning science concepts.

Many of the phenomena in the universe and on earth are guided by elegantly simple relationships. These often appear as dry descriptions and equations in textbooks and in scientific volumes. The computer can bring these things to a level of animation that is the next best thing to reality itself.

The book is not designed for children to use in a drill and practice mode along with their computer. The authors feel that drill and practice is the most trivial use of the computer by children. In this book the program listings allow the child to make use of the computer's special capabilities.

Simulations of satellite motion, ship movement, radar, and sonar are special events which written materials, pictures, and movies cannot convey in an interactive way. The computer programs in this book make possible the interaction.

Don't view the programs in this book as ends in themselves. Most are merely skeletons of ideas. Encourage your children to dress up, modify, and personalize programs for their own needs. Science is not a static project, but rather one on which we build.

1

ARCHITECTURE

PROGRAM

Length, Surface Area, and Volume
Center of Mass

● LENGTH, SURFACE AREA, AND VOLUME

Picture two animals which look the same, but one is twice as tall as the other. Does it have twice as much skin? No, four times as much. Does it weigh twice as much? No, it weighs eight times as much. This is because surface area is related to the length squared, and weight or volume is related to length cubed.

Small animals, like the humingbird, have a lot of surface area compared to their weight. They must eat more than their body weight each day for fuel because they lose heat so quickly from their surface. Likewise, it is easier for a large animal to overheat, since it has a lot of body and relatively little skin from which to lose heat.

This program will show you how surface area and volume of a box of water increase at a rate greater than length increases. The box that appears in the lower-left corner of your screen represents a cube of water which is 1 meter (m) across on each side ($1m^3$) and weighs 2200 pounds.

Program

```
10    REM   LENGTH, SURFACE AREA AND
         VOLUME
20    HOME
30    HGR : HCOLOR= 3
40    DIM P(10,1)
50    FOR C = 0 TO 10
60    READ P(C,0)
70    READ P(C,1)
80    NEXT C
90    DATA   -3,-3,3,-3,3,3,-3,3,-3,
         -3,-1,-4,5,-4,3,-3,3,3,5,1,5
         ,-4
100   F = 1:PX = 10:PY = 149
110    GOSUB 220
120    VTAB (24)
130    INPUT "LENGTH=(0 TO 20 M)? "
         ;L
140   SA = 6 * L ^ 2
150   VO = L ^ 3
160   W = VO * 2200
170   F = L:PX = 120:PY = 90
180    GOSUB 220
190    PRINT "SURFACE AREA=";SA;" M
         ^2"
200    PRINT "VOLUME=";VO;" M^3";"
         WEIGHT=";W;"LBS."
210    END
220    FOR C = 0 TO 9
230    HPLOT PX + F * P(C,0),PY + F
         * P(C,1) TO PX + F * P(C +
         1,0),PY + F * P(C + 1,1)
240    NEXT C
250    RETURN
```

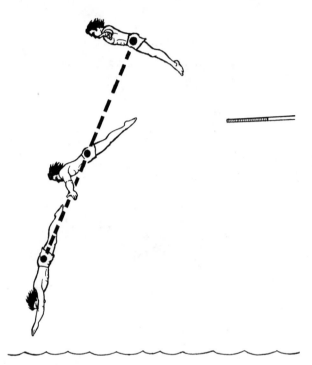

● CENTER OF MASS

The center of mass of a dagger is that point around which the dagger turns when thrown. A seesaw is balanced at its center of mass.

You can use this program to draw any object you wish. Move the cursor around by pressing the cursor arrows. Press [D] to draw a box where the cursor is. Once you have finished drawing, press [C]. The Apple will compute where the center of mass is and place a magenta box there on the screen.

Try this experiment. Stand with your back and heels against a wall. Try to lean forward without moving your feet. You can't, huh? This is because the center of mass must be above your feet for you to keep your balance.

The program can also be used to decide where to place the water fountain in your school so that the student body takes the least steps to get there. Draw a map of the school. Place a box at each classroom. The Apple will place a magenta box where the water fountain should be.

Program

```
10   REM   CENTER OF MASS
20   HOME
30 MOMENT = 0
40 F = 0
50 TF = 0
60   DIM A(39,39)
70 X = 20:Y = 20
80   GR
90 AR =   PEEK ( - 16384): POKE  -
     16368,0: REM   READS KEYBOARD


100   IF Y = 0 THEN 120
110   IF AR = 139 THEN Y = Y - 1
120   IF Y = 39 THEN 140
130   IF AR = 138 THEN Y = Y + 1
140   IF X = 39 THEN 160
150   IF AR = 149 THEN X = X + 1
160   IF X = 0 THEN 180
170   IF AR = 136 THEN X = X - 1
180   COLOR= 15: PLOT X,Y
190   FOR T = 1 TO 100: NEXT T
200   COLOR= 0: PLOT X,Y
210   IF A(X,Y) = 1 THEN   COLOR= 1
     3: PLOT X,Y
220   IF AR = 195 THEN 280: REM   C
     ALCULATE MODE
230   IF AR = 196 THEN 250: REM   D
     RAW MODE
240   GOTO 90
250 A(X,Y) = 1
260   COLOR= 0: PLOT X,Y
270   GOTO 90
280   FOR X = 0 TO 39
290   FOR Y = 0 TO 39
300   IF A(X,Y) = 1 THEN F = F + 1
     :TF = TF + 1
310   NEXT Y
```

```
320 MO = MO + F * X
330 F = 0
340  NEXT X
350 XX = MO / TF
360 MO = 0
370 TF = 0
380  FOR Y = 0 TO 39
390  FOR X = 0 TO 39
400  IF A(X,Y) = 1 THEN F = F + 1
     :TF = TF + 1
410  NEXT X
420 MO = MO + F * Y
430 F = 0
440  NEXT Y
450 YY = MO / TF
460  COLOR= 1: PLOT XX,YY
```

2

ASTRONOMY AND SPACE

PROGRAM

Docking
Encke's Comet
Mercury's Orbit
Inner Planets
Satellite Launch from Earth
Satellite
Three-Stage Rocket

● DOCKING

Dock your personal space module in the mother ship before your fuel runs out. Pressing an arrow key runs a rocket engine in the module and causes you to accelerate (speed up) in that direction. When you are not pressing a key, the rockets are turned off. Since there is no air friction in space to slow you down, your module continues in the same direction with the same speed when the rockets are off. Fire a rocket in the opposite direction to slow down. Good luck!

In the seventeenth century, Sir Isaac Newton described in his Law of Inertia the tendency of moving or still objects to keep doing what they are doing.

Program

```
10   HOME
20   VTAB (10)
30   PRINT "DOCK YOUR SPACE MODULE
         BEFORE FUEL RUNS"
40   PRINT "OUT. ARROW KEYS CONTRO
        L ROCKET ENGINES."
50   VTAB (15): INVERSE
60   PRINT "PRESS ANY KEY."
70   NORMAL
80   GET A$
90   PRINT A$
100   HGR2 : HCOLOR= 3
110 X = 230:Y = 130:VX = 0:VY = 0

120   HPLOT 69,88 TO 64,88 TO 60,9
        0 TO 64,92 TO 78,92 TO 79,93
         TO 83,93 TO 83,87 TO 82,87 TO
        85,83 TO 80,84 TO 77,88 TO 7
        4,88
130   FOR T = 0 TO 100
140 A =   PEEK ( - 16384): POKE  -
       16368,0
150 VX = VX + (A = 149) - (A = 13
       6)
160 VY = VY + (A = 138) - (A = 13
       9)
170 X = X + VX
180 Y = Y + VY
190   HCOLOR= 5
200   HPLOT X,Y TO X + 1,Y
210   IF X < 77 AND X > 64 AND Y <
       92 AND Y > 88 THEN   END
220   FOR Z = 1 TO 500: NEXT Z
230   HCOLOR= 0
240   HPLOT X,Y TO X + 1,Y
250   NEXT T
```

● ENCKE'S COMET

Most comets travel around the sun in elliptical (oval-shaped) paths. The time it takes a comet to make a complete orbit is called its period. Encke's Comet has a very short period of 3.3 years. Halley's Comet has a period of 76 to 79 years. The Comet Tago-Sato-Kosaka has a period of 420,000 years.

Notice how the comet speeds up as it gets closer to the sun and then whips around it.

Program

```
10   REM   ENCKE'S COMET
20   HOME
30 R = 3.14:I = 210:J = 95
40   HGR : HCOLOR= 3
50   HPLOT I,J - 1 TO I,J + 1 TO I
     ,J TO I - 1,J TO I + 1,J
60   FOR T = 0 TO 40
70   VTAB (23): PRINT "MONTH ";T
80 X = 100 *  COS (R) + 140
90 Y = 50 *  SIN (R) + 95
100  HPLOT X,Y
110 D = (((X - I) ^ 2) + ((Y - J)
     ^ 2)) ^ .5
120 R = R + 150 / D ^ 1.5
130  NEXT T
```

● MERCURY'S ORBIT

Mercury is the smallest planet and the one closest to the sun. It has a diameter two-fifths that of the Earth's diameter. Because of its small size and nearness to the bright sun, it is hard to see it from Earth without a telescope.

Mercury moves around the sun faster than any other planet. It goes around the sun in about 88 earth days. The Romans named it Mercury in honor of the swift messenger of their gods.

Mercury's orbit around the sun is shaped like an ellipse. It is 29 million miles from the sun at its closest point and 43 million miles at its farthest point. It travels faster when it is closest to the sun. It was Johannes Keppler who stated in the sixteenth century that planets closer to the sun move the fastest. A form of his equation is found in Line 150 of the program. R is the angle of revolution in radians and D is the distance to the sun.

Program

```
10   REM   MERCURY'S ORBIT
20   HOME
30   HGR : HCOLOR= 3
40 I = 140:J = 80:R = 0:Q = 0
50   HPLOT I,J TO I + 1,J TO I,J +
     1 TO I - 1,J TO I,J - 1
60   FOR T = 0 TO 87
70 X = 75 *  COS (R) + 129
80 Y = 60 *  SIN (R) + 80
90   VTAB (23): PRINT "DAY ";T
100 Q = Q + 1
110   IF T <  > 0 AND Q <  > 5 THEN
      140
120   IF Q = 5 THEN Q = 0
130   HPLOT X,Y
140 D = ((X - I) ^ 2 + (J - Y) ^
     2) ^ .5
150 R = R + 40 / (D ^ 1.5)
160   NEXT T
```

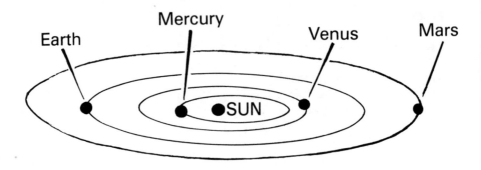

● INNER PLANETS

Our solar system is an orderly mixture of one star, nine known planets, at least 36 moons, thousands of asteroids, and billions of meteoroids and comets. We will look at our star named the sun and the four inner planets called Mercury, Venus, Earth, and Mars.

Mercury is the planet closest to the sun. It travels the fastest of the three planets, circling the sun in 88 earth days. Venus is next. It circles the sun in 224 earth days. Earth circles the sun once a year, or in 365 days. Mars takes 687 days to revolve around the sun.

Notice how the orbits of Earth, Venus, and Mars are almost circular. Mercury has an off-center oval orbit. It travels faster when it is closest to the sun.

The speeds of the planets in this computer program are related in Lines 250 to 280 to a relationship discovered by Johannes Keppler in the sixteenth century. He stated that the time it takes a planet to revolve around the sun is longer the farther it is from the sun. Pluto, the planet farthest from the sun, takes 248 earth years to travel around the sun.

Program

```
10   REM   INNER PLANETS
20   HOME
30 I = 140:J = 80
40 R = 0:RV = 0:RE = 0:RM = 0
50   HGR : HCOLOR= 3
60   HPLOT I + 1,J TO I - 1,J TO I
     ,J TO I,J + 1 TO I,J - 1
70   FOR T = 0 TO 365
80   HCOLOR= 0
90   HPLOT X,Y: HPLOT XV,YV: HPLOT
     XE,YE: HPLOT XM,YM
100 X = 18 *   COS (R) + I - 3
110 Y = 17 *   SIN (R) + J
120 XV = 33.5 *   COS (RV) + I
130 YV = 33.5 *   SIN (RV) + J
140 XE = 46.5 *   COS (RE) + I
150 YE = 46.5 *   SIN (RE) + J
160 XM = 70.8 *   COS (RM) + I - 6

170 YM = 70.8 *   SIN (RM) + J
180   HCOLOR= 3
190   VTAB (23): PRINT "EARTH-DAY
     ";T
200   HPLOT X,Y: HPLOT XV,YV: HPLOT
     XE,YE: HPLOT XM,YM
210 D = ((X - I) ^ 2 + (Y - J) ^
     2) ^ .5
220 DV = ((XV - I) ^ 2 + (YV - J)
     ^ 2) ^ .5
230 DE = ((XE - I) ^ 2 + (YE - J)
     ^ 2) ^ .5
240 DM = ((XM - I) ^ 2 + (YM - J)
     ^ 2) ^ .5
250 R = R + (5.4 / D ^ 1.5)
260 RV = RV + (5.4 / DV ^ 1.5)
270 RE = RE + (5.4 / DE ^ 1.5)
280 RM = RM + (5.4 / DM ^ 1.5)
290   NEXT T
```

15

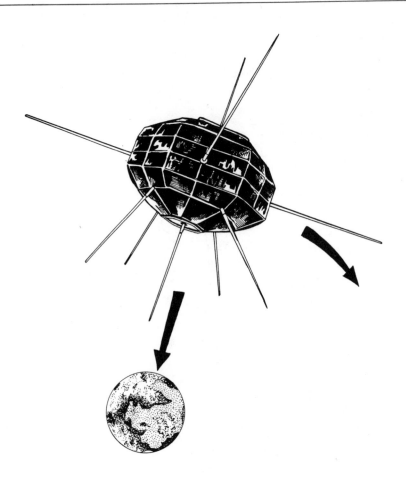

● **SATELLITE**

Toss a satellite around the earth. Decide the altitude and the velocity with which it is launched. Try different combinations of the two to get the types of orbit you wish. If the satellite goes off the screen, it may come back. However, don't wait too long for it to return. It may be years. Or never! Press [Control] and [C] to stop the program.

To orbit the moon, have GV = 20 in Line 20. For a black hole, have GV = 1000 in Line 20. GV is the acceleration due to gravity.

Two laws govern the motion of your satellite. One is the Law of Gravity, which states that the satellite is pulled toward the earth with

16

a force which increases as the satellite gets closer to the earth. The other law is the Law of Inertia. It says that without the force of gravity, the satellite would travel in a straight line with unchanging speed. It is the balance of inertia and gravity which causes the satellite to behave as it does.

Program

```
5   REM  SATELLITE
10   HOME : VTAB 22
20  GV = 100:XE = 140:YE = 80:X1 =
     140:VY = 0
30   INPUT "ALTITUDE (0 TO 80)? ";
     Y1
40   INPUT "VELOCITY (0 TO 10)? ";
     VX
50   HGR
60   HCOLOR= 3
70   HPLOT XE,YE
80  Y1 = Y1 + 80
90   HPLOT X1,160 - Y1
100  GX = XE - X1
110  GY = YE - Y1
120  R = ((GX ^ 2) + (GY ^ 2)) ^ .
     5
130  X2 = X1 + VX + (GV * GX / R ^
     3)
140  Y2 = Y1 + VY + (GV * GY / R ^
     3)
150   IF X2 < 0 OR X2 > 280 OR Y2 <
     0 OR Y2 > 160 THEN 170
160   HPLOT X2,160 - Y2
170  VX = X2 - X1
180  VY = Y2 - Y1
190  X1 = X2
200  Y1 = Y2
210   GOTO 100
```

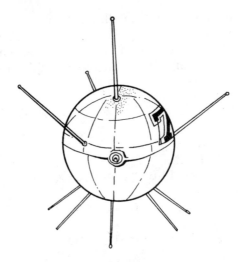

● SATELLITE LAUNCH FROM EARTH

This satellite is launched from the surface of the earth. Set the launch angle (0 to 90 degrees), which is the angle of elevation of the rocket which sends up the satellite. Zero degrees is right along the ground. Ninety degrees is straight up. You also need to give the launch rocket a certain velocity. Don't be surprised if all the satellites that you launch either don't come back or crash back to earth.

Never fear. Your satellites have boosters. After one is launched, wait until the satellite is traveling parallel to earth and then press any key. This will boost the speed of your satellite by 30 percent in the direction it is traveling. With practice, you should become an accomplished satellite launcher. It is a little tricky.

Press [Control] and [C] to stop the program.

Program

```
10  REM   SATELLITE LAUNCH FROM EA
      RTH
20  HOME : VTAB (24)
30  HGR : HCOLOR= 3
40  GV = 200:XE = 140:YE = 80
50  X1 = 140:Y1 = 110
```

```
60   FOR Z = 0 TO 6.28 STEP .04
70 X = 140 + 30 *  COS (Z)
80 Y = 80 + 30 *  SIN (Z)
90   HPLOT X,159 - Y
100   NEXT Z
110   INPUT "DEGREES ELEVATION (0
      TO 90)? ";EL
120   INPUT "VELOCITY (0 TO 5)? ";
      V
130 VX = V *  COS (EL / 180 * 3.1
      4)
140 VY = V *  SIN (EL / 180 * 3.1
      4)
150   IF X1 < 0 OR X1 > 279 OR Y1 <
      0 OR Y1 > 159 THEN 170
160   HPLOT X1,159 - Y1
170 GX = XE - X1
180 GY = YE - Y1
190 R = (GX ^ 2 + GY ^ 2) ^ .5
200 B = 1
210 P =   PEEK ( - 16384): POKE  -
      16368,0
220   IF P > 127 THEN B = 1.3
230 X2 = X1 + B * VX + (GV * GX /
      R ^ 3)
240 Y2 = Y1 + B * VY + (GV * GY /
      R ^ 3)
250 GX = XE - X1
260 VX = X2 - X1
270 VY = Y2 - Y1
280 X1 = X2
290 Y1 = Y2
300   GOTO 150
```

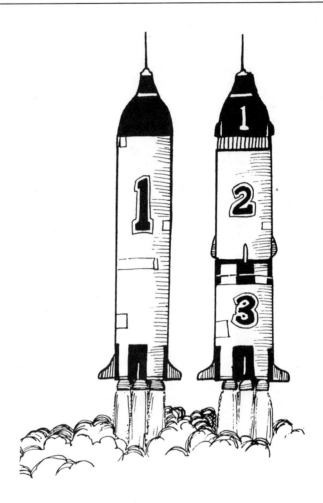

● THREE-STAGE ROCKET

The Apple will compare flight statistics from a one-stage rocket and a three-stage rocket. Both are the same size and weight, carry the same amount of fuel, and have engines that develop the same thrust. Both rockets have two-thirds their weight in fuel at the start. However, the three-stage rocket can "drop" each stage as the stage runs out of fuel. The rocket doesn't carry the extra weight around.

Let's compare the altitude and speed of each rocket after they blast off at the same time.

Program

```
10   REM  THREE STAGE ROCKET
20   HOME : SPEED= 175
30 R(0) = 180:R(1) = 180
40 F(0) = 420:F(1) = 420
50 T(0) = 0
60 A(0) = 0:A(1) = 0
70 V(0) = 0:V(1) = 0
80 L(0) = 5000:L(1) = 5000
90 Z = 0
100 M(Z) = R(Z) + F(Z)
110 T(Z) = T(Z) + 1
120   IF F(Z) < 1 THEN F(Z) = 1: GOTO
      140
130 A(Z) = L(Z) / M(Z)
140   IF F(Z) = 1 THEN A(Z) = 0
150 V(Z) = V(Z) + A(Z)
160 Y(Z) = Y(Z) + V(Z)
170 F(Z) = F(Z) - 5
180   IF Z = 1 AND F(1) = 210 THEN
      R(1) = R(1) - 90: PRINT : PRINT
       SPC( 19): INVERSE : PRINT "
      STAGE 1 SEPARATION": NORMAL
      : PRINT
190   IF Z = 1 AND F(1) = 70 THEN
      R(1) = R(1) - 60: PRINT : PRINT
       SPC( 19): INVERSE : PRINT "
      STAGE 2 SEPARATION": NORMAL
      : PRINT
200   IF Z = 0 THEN  PRINT : PRINT
       TAB( 13)T(0);" SECONDS": PRINT

210   IF Z = 0 AND F(Z) < 1 THEN 2
      30
220   GOTO 240
230   INVERSE : PRINT "0 FUEL": NORMAL
      : SPEED= 255: END
240   IF Z = 0 THEN  PRINT  INT (Y
      (Z));" FEET"
```

21

```
250   IF Z = 1 THEN  PRINT  TAB( 2
      0) INT (Y(Z));" FEET"
260   IF Z = 0 THEN  PRINT  INT (V
      (Z));" FEET/SECOND"
270   IF Z = 1 THEN  PRINT  TAB( 2
      0) INT (V(Z));" FEET/SECOND"

280   IF Z = 1 THEN Z = 0: GOTO 30
      0
290   IF Z = 0 THEN Z = 1
300   GOTO 100
310   PRINT  SPC( 13): INVERSE : PRINT
      "STAGE 1 SEPARATION": NORMAL

320   SPEED= 255
```

3

BIOLOGY

PROGRAMS

Grass Stem Growth
Woody Stem Growth
Population Forecast
Sex Probability
What to Plant Where?
Cone Shell Growth
Cowry Shell Growth
Pond Farming

● GRASS STEM GROWTH

The grass always seems to grow back after we mow the lawn. This is because the active growing part of the stem is near the level of the soil. It keeps pushing up new stem.

Have fun watching the grass grow. See how the older parts of the stem wind up toward the top of the plant.

Other plants with parallel veins in their leaves and one cotyledon in their seeds grow this way. Some examples are lily, banana, and grain plants.

Program

```
10    REM   GRASS STEM GROWTH
20    HOME
30    PRINT   TAB( 15)"GRASS STEM"
40  X = 20:Y =   - 1
50    FOR T = 1 TO 9
60    FOR Z = 1 TO 1000: NEXT Z
70    FOR N = T TO 1 STEP   - 1
80  Y = Y + 1
90    VTAB (23 - Y)
100   PRINT   TAB( X);
110   INVERSE
120   PRINT N: NORMAL
130   NEXT N
140 Y =   - 1
150   NEXT T
```

● WOODY STEM GROWTH

Woody stems grow from the tip. This means that new plant is added on near the top end. The oldest part of the stem is near the base of the plant.

Trees and other woody plants also grow in width. The oldest part of the stem is in the center; the youngest is toward the outside. Each tree ring marks one year of growth.

Program

```
10   REM   WOODY STEM GROWTH
20   HOME
30   PRINT   TAB( 15)"WOODY STEM"
40 X = 20
50   FOR Y = 1 TO 9
60   FOR Z = 1 TO 1000: NEXT Z
70   VTAB (23 - Y)
80   PRINT   TAB( X);: INVERSE : PRINT
     Y: NORMAL
90   NEXT Y
```

● POPULATION FORECAST

The number of people living in an area is its population. Populations grow faster in different parts of the world.

The table below shows the populations and their growth rates for the world and all the continents except Antarctica.

Area	Population	Population per square mile	Yearly growth	Doubling time in years
World	4,600,000,000	—	1.9%	37
Asia	2,493,000,000	148	2.1%	34
Africa	452,000,000	39	2.6%	27
Europe	684,000,000	168	0.6%	119
North America	364,000,000	39	0.9%	77
South America	237,000,000	34	2.7%	26
Australia	14,000,000	5	1.5%	46

This program will help you forecast the population in an area in which you are interested for any year in the future. For instance, how many more people may live in Asia in the year 2000? In your home town? One # represents the population today.

Change the year in Line 70 to the present year if it is not current.

Program

```
10   REM   POPULATION FORECAST
20   HOME
30   INPUT "THE POPULATION WILL TA
     KE HOW MANY YEARS TO DOUBLE?
      ";YD
40   PRINT
50   INPUT "YEAR IN QUESTION? ";Y
60   PRINT
70 D = Y - 1983
80 YG =   EXP ( LOG (2) / YD)
90 NU = YG ^ D
100   FOR P = 0 TO NU
110   PRINT "#";
120   NEXT P
130   PRINT
140   PRINT : PRINT "IN ";Y;" THE
      POPULATION WILL BE"
150   PRINT NU;" TIMES TODAY'S."
```

● SEX PROBABILITY

Probability and chance are the same thing. When a child is born, there is one chance in two that it will be the male sex (a boy). The probability is ½. Likewise, there is one chance in two that it will be the female sex (a girl) and the probability is ½. The probability that a family will have a boy first and then a girl is ½ × ½ = ¼. The probability for two girls is ½ × ½ = ¼. We multiply the probabilities for each child together to get a combined probability.

It gets a little bit more complicated if we don't care which sex (male or female) comes first in a family. For instance, the births in a family with two children could be (a) boy, boy; (b) boy, girl; (c) girl, boy; or (d) girl, girl. Only (b) and (c) families have a boy and a girl. There are then two chances in four, or a probability of ½, of having a family with one boy and one girl.

In this program you input the number of boys and girls that you wish to have in your family. The Apple will "make" 1000 families of the same size as yours. Then it will print out the number of families that had the same number of boys and girls as yours.

Remember, the bigger the family size, the longer it will take the 1000 families to have their babies.

Program

```
10   REM   SEX PROBABILITY
20   HOME
30   VTAB (7)
40   PRINT "CHILDREN IN ONE FAMILY
     ?"
50   PRINT : INPUT "GIRLS? ";G
60   INPUT "BOYS? ";B
70 N = G + B
80   PRINT : PRINT "1000 FAMILIES
     ARE NOW HAVING"
90   PRINT N;" BABY(S) EACH."
100 CC = 0
110  FOR Q = 1 TO 1000
120 C = 0
130  FOR R = 1 TO N
140 GI =   RND (1)
150  IF GI < .5 THEN C = C + 1
160  NEXT R
170  IF C = G THEN CC = CC + 1
180  NEXT Q
190  PRINT : PRINT CC;" FAMILIES
     HAD ";G;" GIRL(S) & ";B;" BO
     Y(S).
200 S =   - 16336: REM   BUZZ
210  FOR Z = 1 TO 20:SO =   PEEK (
     S): NEXT Z
```

● WHAT TO PLANT WHERE?

The TV monitor represents an aerial view of a field which you are going to farm. The soil at the top of the screen is wet; at the center of the screen, moist; and at the bottom of the screen, dry. This is defined in Lines 60, 70, and 80. The left side of the field is dark; the center, shaded; and the right side, bright (Lines 90, 100, and 110). Lines 120 to 150 show the ideal growing conditions for plants M, F, and T. Line 170 prints an M, F, or T where they should be grown. The Apple must make a decision of *what* to grow, if anything, at every location in the field.

You can customize this program for your home garden. It will help you decide what to grow where.

Program

```
10   REM  WHAT TO PLANT WHERE
20   HOME
30   FOR X = 40 TO 1 STEP  - 1
40   FOR Y = 1 TO 22
50   REM  FIELD CONDITIONS
60   IF Y < 7 THEN M$ = "WET"
70   IF Y >  = 7 AND Y < 11 THEN M
     $ = "MOIST"
80   IF Y >  = 11 THEN M$ = "DRY"
90   IF X < 4 THEN S$ = "DARK"
100   IF X >  = 4 AND X < 19 THEN
     S$ = "SHADE"
110   IF X >  = 19 THEN S$ = "BRIG
     HT"
120  L$ = " "
130   IF M$ = "WET" AND S$ = "DARK
     " THEN L$ = "M"
140   IF M$ = "WET" AND S$ = "SHAD
     E" THEN L$ = "F"
150   IF M$ = "MOIST" AND S$ = "BR
     IGHT" THEN L$ = "T"
160  VTAB (Y)
170  PRINT  TAB( X)L$
180  NEXT Y
190  NEXT X
```

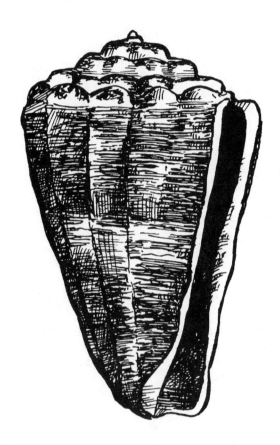

● **CONE SHELL GROWTH**

The cone shell is part of a marine animal called a gastropod which has a flattened, muscular, creeping foot. The shell is a tube which increases in size as it winds in a spiral. Each turn, or whorl, is slightly larger than the one before. The tip, or apex, of the shell is where the tiny animal started to grow. You can see an apex at the top of the picture above. You will be watching the shell grow on the video screen with a view directly on this apex.

Program

```
10   REM   CONE SHELL GROWTH
20   HGR2 : HCOLOR= 3
30  CX = 140:CY = 95:RA = 0:R = 0
40   FOR RE = 0 TO 15 * 3.14 STEP
      3.14 / 50
50  R = R + .0002
60  RA = RA + R
70  X = CX + RA *   COS (RE)
80  Y = CY + RA *   SIN (RE)
90   HPLOT X,Y
100   NEXT RE
```

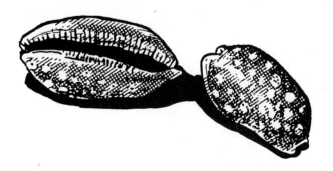

● **COWRY SHELL GROWTH**

The cowry is a shelled animal that lives in the ocean. It lives inside its shell. The cowry can extend the part of its body called the mantle to the outside of its shell. The mantle takes chemicals from the ocean and cements them to the outside of the shell. This is the way that the shell gets bigger.

As the animal gets bigger, it must wear away the inside of the shell to make room for its larger body.

Line 120 builds up the outside of the shell. Line 170 wears away the inside of the shell.

Program

```
10   REM   COWRY SHELL GROWTH
20   HOME : HGR
30 TH = 3
40   FOR B = 13 TO 30
50   FOR C = 1 TO B ^ 2
60 A =   RND (1) * 5.235
70 AN = A + 5.235
80 R = B - ( ABS (AN - 7.854) * 4
     )
90 X =   COS (AN) * R + 140
100 Y =   SIN (AN) * R + 80
110   HCOLOR= 3
120   HPLOT X,159 - Y
130   IF B > 23 THEN TH = 4
```

```
140 S =   COS (AN) * (R - TH) + 14
     0
150 T =   SIN (AN) * (R - TH) + 80

160   HPLOT S,159 - T
170   IF AN  = 5.4 THEN  HCOLOR=
      0: HPLOT S,159 - T
180   NEXT C
190   NEXT B
```

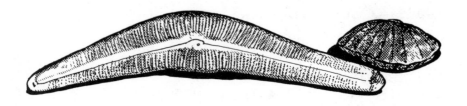

A microscopic alga magnified many times next to an oyster.

● POND FARMING

An alga (one is an *alga*, two or more are *algae*) is a water plant. Algae can be microscopic like the diatom in the picture above or as tall as a tree. An oyster is a shelled animal that lives in sea water and eats microscopic algae such as diatoms.

Aquaculture is the farming of water plants and animals. This computer program will let you test your aquaculture skill. The idea is to grow as much algae as you can in the 50 days before oyster spat (babies) arrive.

Start with a billion-liter pond which is empty except for 1000 liters of nutrient water with 1 liter of concentrated algae mixed in. You will be adding nutrient water over a period of 50 days and watching the amount of algae increase or decrease.

This exercise can be frustrating. Here are some things to keep in mind to help you be a successful farmer.

1. Algae only reproduce and grow if conditions are right.

2. Algae, like birds and people, can change their environment to make conditions right. Birds build nests. People build homes. Algae make chemicals which they release into the water to make growing conditions better for them.

3. If there is a lot of nutrient water and very few algae, it will take a long time for the algae to change their environment. They may die off before they do it.

4. If there is little nutrient water and many algae, then the algae will run out of food and also pollute their water environment.

5. So, you must find the right balance of algae and nutrient water to grow the most algae. Watch your concentration carefully and find the concentration that works the best.

6. Under optimum (the best) conditions, the algae population will double over the same period of time. This means that each day you must add more nutrient water than you did the day before.

Good luck, aquaculturist. Keep a log so that you can learn from your successes and failures. Challenge a friend to do better than you did.

The program begins on the following page.

Note: Line 270 contains the master equation for growth. C = concentration of algae. The greatest rate of growth is 1.3 times the previous day's concentration.

Program

```
20    TEXT : HOME
30    PRINT  TAB( 11)"POND FARMING"

40    PRINT : PRINT
50    PRINT "GROW A LARGE YIELD OF
      ALGAE. YOUR"
60    PRINT "CULTURE NOW HAS ONE LI
      TER (L) OF"
70    PRINT "CONCENTRATED ALGAE IN
      1000 L OF WATER."
80    PRINT "THE POND CAN HOLD ONE
      BILLION L. YOU"
90    PRINT "HAVE 50 DAYS TO GROW A
      LGAE BEFORE"
100   PRINT "OYSTER SPAT ARRIVE. A
      DD NUTRIENT WATER"
110   PRINT "AT AN OPTIMUM RATE."
120   PRINT : PRINT
130   INVERSE : PRINT "PRESS ANY K
      EY.": NORMAL
140   GET Q$
150 A = 1:V = 1000:FL = 0:C = .00
      1:D = 0
160 R = 10 ^ 9:M = 0:Z = 50
170   HGR : HOME : VTAB (24)
180   INPUT "L OF NUTRIENT WATER T
      O ADD?";FL
190 V = V + FL
200   IF V > 10 ^ 9 THEN 410
210   INPUT "DAYS TO GROW? ";D
220   IF D > Z THEN 440
230 Z = Z - D
240   FOR T = 1 TO D
250 C = A / V
260   IF C < = 0 THEN 600
```

```
270  C = C * (1.3 - ((( LOG (C) +
     11.5) ^ 2) * .02))
280   IF C < 0 THEN C = 0
290  A = V * C
300  R = (10 ^ 9) - V
310   NEXT T
320   HOME : VTAB (22): PRINT "L A
     LGAE=";A;
330   PRINT  SPC( 4)"TOTAL L=";V
340   PRINT "DAYS LEFT=";Z
350   PRINT "L ALGAE/1000000 L WAT
     ER=";C * 1000000
360   GOSUB 470
370   IF Z <  = 0 THEN 460
380  T = 0:FL = 0:D = 0
390   GOTO 180
400   GOTO 290
410   PRINT "DO NOT OVERFLOW"
420  V = V - FL
430   GOTO 180
440   PRINT "TOO MANY DAYS"
450   GOTO 210
460   PRINT "OYSTER SPAT ARRIVED."
     : INVERSE : PRINT "PRESS ANY
      KEY FOR STATISITCS.": NORMAL
     : GET A$: TEXT : END
470   IF A <  = 0 THEN 600
480   HGR
490   HCOLOR= 3: HPLOT 0,50 TO 15,
     50 TO 15,153 TO 269,153 TO 2
     69,50 TO 279,50
500 HT = 100 * (V / 10 ^ 9)
510   HCOLOR= 1
520   HPLOT 16,152 - HT TO 268,152
      - HT
530   HCOLOR= 1
540   FOR N = 1 TO A / 100
550 X =  RND (1) * 253 + 16
```

```
560 Y = 152 - HT +  RND (1) * HT
570  HPLOT X,Y
580  NEXT N
590  RETURN
600  PRINT "DEAD POND"
610  END
```

4

CHEMISTRY

PROGRAMS

Diffusion
Tevatron

● DIFFUSION

Diffusion in chemistry is the mixing of atoms or molecules of one fluid with those of another fluid. The fluid can be either a gas or a liquid. Diffusion is caused by the natural, random movement of atoms and molecules, and not by stirring, shaking, or blowing. Odors from perfume, food, and other sources are produced by the diffusion of gaseous odor molecules with molecules of air.

Have a friend open a bottle of perfume in a room with no drafts. Determine how long it takes you to smell the perfume at the other side of the room. Or, put a drop of ink or food coloring in a glass of water and watch the color diffuse into the water.

Your video monitor will show the motion of 31 molecules whose X and Y positions are set at 140 and 80 respectively in Lines 40 to 60. The loop from Lines 70 through 180 moves the molecules. Lines 80 and 90 change the X and Y positions of each molecule a random number between +15 and -15. The old position is erased in Line 120 and the new position plotted in Line 170.

The unrealistic part is that only one molecule moves at a time, instead of all the molecules at once as it should be.

44

Program

```
10   REM   DIFFUSION
20   HOME : HGR
30   DIM A(30,1)
40   FOR N = 0 TO 30
50 A(N,0) = 140:A(N,1) = 80
60   NEXT N
70   FOR N = 0 TO 30
80 DX = 15 -   RND (1) * 30
90 DY = 15 -   RND (1) * 30
100 X = A(N,0):Y = A(N,1)
110   IF X < 0 OR X > 279 OR Y < 0
      OR Y > 159 THEN   GOTO 130
120   HCOLOR= 0: HPLOT X,Y
130 A(N,0) = A(N,0) + DX
140 A(N,1) = A(N,1) + DY
150 X = A(N,0):Y = A(N,1)
160   IF X < 0 OR X > 279 OR Y < 0
      OR Y > 159 THEN   GOTO 180
170   HCOLOR= 3: HPLOT X,Y
180   NEXT N
190   GOTO 70
```

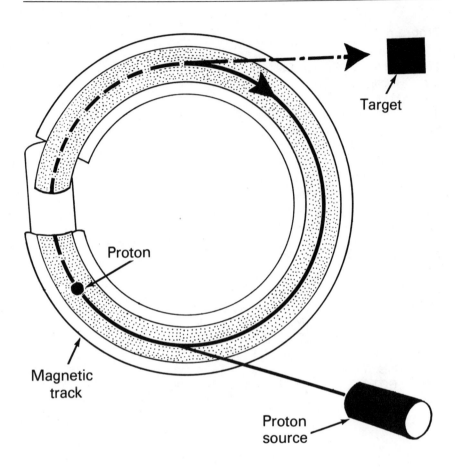

Target

Proton

Magnetic
track

Proton
source

● TEVATRON

The tevatron is a giant atom smasher located outside of the city of Chicago. It is really a circular track four miles around which is lined with electromagnets. The magnets speed up parts of atoms called protons around the track until the protons almost reach the speed of light (186,000 miles per second). That means the protons whirl around the track about 50,000 times a second. Pretty fast, huh?

When these high-speed protons strike a target (for example, a metal bar), they shatter its atoms, giving off a shower of pieces of atoms. Scientists use detection devices to study the trails left by the atomic pieces to figure out how atoms work.

This program makes a proton accelerate or speed up in a circular path. A picture is taken of the proton's position every split second. Lines 100 and 110 contain the equations for a circle. The radius is 75, and at the center of the circle X = 140 and Y = 80.

Have a smashing time. Don't get dizzy. We let the Apple slow down the proton so you can see it.

Program

```
10   REM   TEVATRON
20   HOME
30   HGR
40 A = 0
50 C = 75
60 CX = 140:CY = 80
70   FOR T = 1 TO 11 STEP .01
80 A = A + .5
90 R = A * T
100 X = C *  COS (R) + CX
110 Y = C *  SIN (R) + CY
120   HCOLOR= 3: HPLOT X,Y
130   FOR Z = 1 TO 5: NEXT Z
140   HCOLOR= 0: HPLOT X,Y
150   NEXT T
160   TEXT
```

5

DATA MANAGEMENT

PROGRAMS

Bar Graph
Point Plotter
Minimum, Maximum, and Mean
Classification
Label Maker
Alphabetic Sort

● **BAR GRAPH**

A bar graph can make your data easier to understand.

Put in your own data starting at Line 190. Enter a single-letter label, then a number, then a label, then a letter, etc. A total of 20 bars will fit on the screen. Only positive numbers can be used.

After your last letter and number enter END. The Apple will make the largest bar 38 spaces tall, with the rest of the bars of proportional length.

The graph described by the data in the listing represents the time a student spends studying each month.

Program

```
10   REM   BAR GRAPH
20 MX = 0:C =   - 1
30   HOME : GR : COLOR= 15
40   DIM L$(39): DIM Y(21)
50   READ L$
60   IF L$ = "END" THEN 120
70   READ Y
80   IF Y > MX THEN MX = Y
90 C = C + 1
100 L$(C) = L$:Y(C) = Y
110   GOTO 50
120   FOR X = 0 TO C
130   PRINT L$(X);" ";
140   FOR Y = 39 TO (39 - (Y(X) /
     MX) * 38) STEP  - 1
150   PLOT 2 * X,Y
160   NEXT Y
170   NEXT X
180   PRINT
190   DATA  J,90,F,100,M,95,A,90,M
     ,80,J,75
200   DATA  J,15,A,10,S,69,O,85,N,
     90,D,95,END
```

● POINT PLOTTER

This program was built to make graphing data points easy. The Apple will plot the data points and show minimum and maximum values.

What do you have to do? All the work is in the data starting in Line 320. Use your own data. Enter the X value for the first point, Y value for the first point, X value for the second point, Y value for the second point, etc. After the last X and Y values, key in 999. This lets the Apple know that there are no more data points. Then run the program to draw the graph.

Program

```
10    REM   POINT PLOTTER
20    HGR
30    HCOLOR= 3
40    HOME
50    DIM X(200): DIM Y(200)
60  C =   - 1
70  MX = 0:MY = 0
80  SX = 10 ^ 10:SY = 10 ^ 10
90    HPLOT 0,9 TO 0,159 TO 150,159

100   HPLOT 0,0 TO 3,3 TO 5,0 TO 3
      ,3 TO 3,6
110   HPLOT 155,158 TO 160,153
120   HPLOT 155,153 TO 160,158
130   READ X
140   IF X = 999 THEN 240
150   READ Y
160   IF X > MX THEN MX = X
170   IF Y > MY THEN MY = Y
180   IF X < SX THEN SX = X
190   IF Y < SY THEN SY = Y
200 C = C + 1
210 X(C) = X
220 Y(C) = Y
```

```
230    GOTO 130
240    FOR Z = 0 TO C
250  X = ((X(Z) - SX) / MX) * 150
260  Y = 159 - ((Y(Z) - SY) / MY) *
       150
270    HPLOT X,Y
280    NEXT Z
290    VTAB (24)
300    PRINT "MINIMUM X=";SX;"      ";
       "MAXIMUM X=";MX
310    PRINT "MINIMUM Y=";SY;"      ";
       "MAXIMUM Y=";MY
320    DATA  0,0,11,76,39,67,89,123
       ,59,222,45,98,111,33,999
```

● MINIMUM, MAXIMUM, AND MEAN

Suppose Joan gave you a sheet of paper on which she recorded the weights of 200 newborn rabbits. Then Joan asked you to come to a conclusion regarding the weights of the rabbits. A bunch of data like this can be confusing. You might use *statistics,* which is a branch of mathematics, to simplify the numbers to make them more understandable.

Some of the statistical terms you might use are minimum, maximum, and mean. The minimum value is the smallest value. The maximum is the largest value. The mean is the average value. The mean value is determined by adding up all the values and then dividing that sum by the total number of values.

Let the Apple do the work for you. In Line 150 enter your data numbers. Then enter the number 999 to let the Apple know that there is no more data. Run the program to get your minimum, maximum, and mean values.

Program

```
10   REM   MINIMUM, MAXIMUM AND MEA
     N
20   HOME
30 MX =   - 10 ^ 15:MI = 10 ^ 15:N
     = 0:T = 0
40   READ X
50   IF X = 999 THEN 110
60 N = N + 1
70   IF X > MX THEN MX = X
80   IF X < MI THEN MI = X
90 T = T + X
100   GOTO 40
110 ME = T / N
120   PRINT "MINIMUM VALUE=";MI
130   PRINT "MAXIMUM VALUE=";MX
140   PRINT "MEAN VALUE=";ME
150   DATA  12,34,56,109,87,44,90,
     35,999
```

● CLASSIFICATION

Classification is a method scientists use to arrange things in related groups. The computer can help you keep track of all animals, plants, rocks, or other things you may have seen or collected and classified. For instance, orioles, canaries, and cardinals can be classified as birds.

Enter you data starting on Line 90. After each item, key in a three-letter abbreviation for its class. In the sample data, FIS is fish, INS is insect, BIR is bird. At the end of all your data statements, key in END,END.

Run the program. You can now retrieve a list of any single class you wish.

Program

```
10   REM   CLASSIFICATION
20   HOME
30   INPUT "CLASS? ";CA$
40   PRINT
50   READ I$,C$
60   IF C$ = "END" THEN   END
70   IF  LEFT$ (C$,3) =  LEFT$ (CA
     $,3) THEN   PRINT I$
80   GOTO 50
90   DATA   CARP,FIS,COD,FIS,MOTH,I
     NS,CANARY,BIR,MOLLY,FIS,BUTT
     ERFLY,INS
100  DATA   CARDINAL,BIR,WEEVIL,IN
     S,GUPPY,FIS,BASS,FIS,BEETLE,
     INS,ORIOLE,BIR,END,END
```

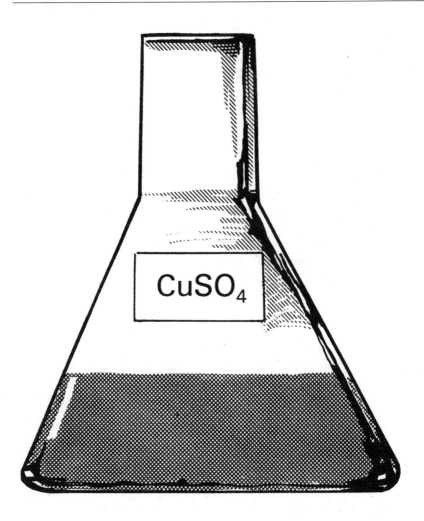

CuSO$_4$

● **LABEL MAKER**

This is the only program in this book that requires a printer. Use this program to make labels for your experiments and collections.

The Apple will ask you what label is to be printed, the number of labels to be printed, and whether or not the labels should be numbered sequentially (1, 2, 3, etc.). Attach your labels to your experiment or collection.

Program

```
10    REM   LABEL MAKER
20    HOME
30    INPUT "LINE 1? ";L1$
40    INPUT "LINE 2? ";L2$
50    INPUT "LINE 3? ";L3$
60    INPUT "NUMBER OF LABELS? ";N
70    INPUT "NUMBERED SEQUENTIALLY
      (Y/N)? ";R$
80    PR# 1
90    FOR Z = 1 TO N
100   PRINT
110   IF R$ = "Y" THEN 140
120   PRINT : PRINT L1$: PRINT L2$
      : PRINT L3$: PRINT
130   GOTO 150
140   PRINT : PRINT L1$;" ";Z: PRINT
      L2$: PRINT L3$: PRINT
150   NEXT Z
160   PR# 0
```

● ALPHABETIC SORT

This is called a "bubble sort" program. The computer logic "floats" words that come early in alphabetic order to the top of the list. Each word is compared to the word above it. If they are in reverse order they switch places. The computer then compares the next lowest word with the one above it.

All words are compared in the loop from Lines 100 to 150. This loop is nested in another loop which repeats the whole process a few less times than there are words. When it is finished, all words are in alphabetic order. Line 180 prints out the list after all the words are sorted. Be patient. The sorting takes a while.

Enter your words starting at Line 200 and finish the data statement with 999 to let the Apple know that there are no more words.

Program

```
10   REM  ALPHABETIC SORT
20   HOME :
30   DIM A$(500)
40 A = 0
50   READ A$(A)
60   IF A$(A) = "999" THEN 90
70 A = A + 1
80   GOTO 50
90   FOR K = 0 TO A - 2
100   FOR Z = 0 TO A - 2
110   IF A$(Z) < A$(Z + 1) THEN 15
      0
120 B$ = A$(Z + 1)
130 A$(Z + 1) = A$(Z)
140 A$(Z) = B$
150   NEXT Z
160   NEXT K
170   FOR Z = 0 TO A - 1
180   PRINT A$(Z)
190   NEXT Z
200   DATA  PUMICE,MICA,GRANITE,AR
      AGONITE,999
```

6

ENERGY BUDGETING

PROGRAMS

Food Conversion
Step Saver

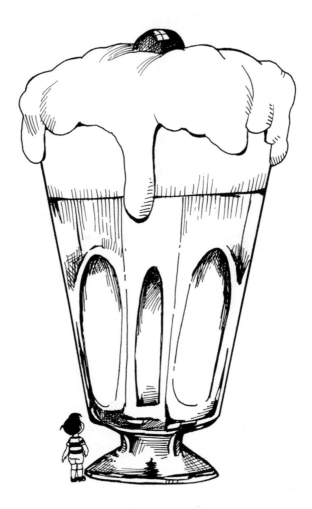

● FOOD CONVERSION

How much food have we eaten in our lifetime? What would all this food look like if it was piled up in one place? The Apple will answer these questions while drawing a pile of food on the screen next to a representation of ourselves. When the Apple draws the picture of the food, it will have no more depth than our own bodies.

If you have eaten 60 times your weight, that means you have a food conversion ratio of 60. Try out this program on your parents.

The program helped the authors realize why it takes so much agriculture to support our eating needs.

A good science project would be to calculate how much more plant material it takes to support a meat-eating person as compared to a vegetarian. Remember that the cow, pig, or fish that we eat had to eat many times its weight in plants.

Program

```
10    REM   FOOD CONVERSION
20    TEXT : HOME
30    PRINT   TAB( 13)"FOOD CONVERSI
      ON"
40    VTAB 5
50    INPUT "AGE IN YEARS? ";YE
60    INPUT "WEIGHT IN POUNDS? ";P
70    PRINT "AVERAGE NUMBER OF POUN
      DS OF FOOD THAT"
80    INPUT "YOU EAT PER DAY? ";F
90 TF = F * 365 * YE
100 D = 3 * ((TF / P) ^ .5)
110   HGR : HCOLOR= 3
120   HPLOT 0,158 TO 0,149
130 XX = D + 7
140   FOR X = 7 TO XX
150   FOR Y = 159 - D TO 159
160   HPLOT X,Y
170   NEXT Y
180   NEXT X
190   VTAB 24
200   PRINT "YOU HAVE EATEN "; INT
      (TF);" POUNDS IN ";YE
210   PRINT "YEARS OR "; INT (TF /
      P);" TIMES YOUR WEIGHT."
220   PRINT "TRY IT AGAIN? (Y/N)
230   GET R$
240   IF R$ = "Y" THEN 10
250   TEXT : HOME : END
```

● STEP SAVER

The function of the program is to help you plan the placement of furniture and appliances in a room measuring 10 steps by 10 steps so that you will take the least number of walking steps in your normal daily routine.

There will be 16 locations in the room. You don't have to use all of them. Assign two letters for each piece of furniture or appliance or space. Then decide which sequence you might follow in the room. For instance, refrigerator (RE) to stove (ST) to oven (OV) to window (WI) etc. Start the sequence in the data Line 440 and end the data with END.

Run the program. The Apple will ask you which letter to put in each location. If, for example, location No. 4 has a refrigerator, enter (RE) and then press [Return].

After all 16 locations are filled, the Apple will count the steps it would take to walk through your sequence. Run the program again with another arrangement, trying for more step-saving efficiency.

Program

```
10    REM   STEP SAVER
20    DIM A(15,1)
30    HOME
40 N = 0
50    FOR Y = 1 TO 4
60    FOR X = 1 TO 4
70 N = N + 1
80 A(N - 1,1) = Y
90 A(N - 1,0) = X
100   VTAB (5 - Y) * 5
110   PRINT  TAB( (5 - X) * 5)N
120   NEXT X
130   NEXT Y
140   DIM A$(15)
150   FOR N = 1 TO 16
160   VTAB 23
170   PRINT "LOCATION ";N;
180   INPUT A$(N - 1)
190 X = A(N - 1,0)
200 Y = A(N - 1,1)
210   VTAB (5 - Y) * 5
220   PRINT  TAB( (5 - X) * 5)A$(N
      - 1)
230   VTAB 23: PRINT "
          "
240   NEXT N
250 T = 1:D = 0
260   READ Q$
270   IF Q$ = "END" THEN 430
280   FOR N = 1 TO 16
290   IF Q$ < > A$(N - 1) THEN 33
      0
300 X = A(N - 1,0)
310 Y = A(N - 1,1)
320   GOTO 340
330   NEXT N
340   IF T < > 1 THEN 380
```

```
350 T = T + 1
360 XX = A(N - 1,0)
370 YY = A(N - 1,1)
380 F = ((X - XX) ^ 2 + (Y - YY) ^
    2) ^ .5
390 D = D + F
400 XX = X
410 YY = Y
420   GOTO 260
430   PRINT D;" STEPS"
440   DATA  RE,ST,OV,WI,END
```

7

HYDRAULICS

PROGRAM

River Flow

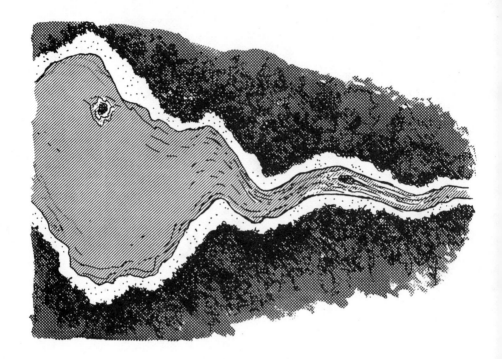

● RIVER FLOW

This is a demonstration program which shows the speed of flowing river water. The flow of water through a river bed or through a pipe is defined as the volume of water that passes through a section of the river or pipe in a certain amount of time. Flow can be expressed as cubic meters per second or gallons per second. If there are no extra outlets, the flow is the same along a number of sections of river or pipe. If a river narrows and becomes shallower, the flow remains the same. But, the speed of the water at that section must be faster to get the same volume of water through in the same time.

Program

```
10   REM   RIVER FLOW
20   HOME
30   HGR : HCOLOR= 3
40   FOR X = 0 TO 279
50   GOSUB 170
60   HPLOT X,Y
70   HPLOT X,YY
80   NEXT X
90   HCOLOR= 2
100   FOR X = 0 TO 279
110   GOSUB 170
120   FOR A = YY TO Y
130   HPLOT X,A
140   NEXT A
150   NEXT X
160   VTAB 23: END
170 Y = 100 + 20 *   SIN (.05 * X)

180 YY = 60 + 15 *   SIN (.02 * X)

190   RETURN
```

8

INSTRUMENTATION

PROGRAM

Stroboscope

● STROBOSCOPE

A stroboscope is an instrument that gives off many split-second flashes cf light per second. You may have seen "strobes" at school dances and at discos. They make the dancers appear to have short, jerky motions. This is because we only see the dancers during the light flashes.

A stroboscope can make swiftly turning machinery or an insect's fluttering wing seem to stand still. This will happen only if the stroboscope's flash rate is set so that it flashes only when the machinery or wing returns to the same position.

This program is short, but flashy! Line 20 asks you to input the number of flashes per second. Press [Control] and [C] to stop the strobe.

Use your stroboscope to figure out how fast a top or motor spins. Or, take a time-exposed camera picture in a blackened room of something moving, such as a falling ball. Use your stroboscope as a source of light. Many images will appear on your photograph. Use a fast film (ISO 1000) for this picture.

Program

```
10   REM   STROBOSCOPE
20   HOME : INPUT "FLASHES/SECOND?
       ";F
30   HGR : POKE  - 16302,0: REM   F
     ULL SCREEN
40   HGR2
50   REM   CHANGE HGR2 TO WHITE
60   FOR I = 16384 TO 24575: POKE
     I,255 -   PEEK (I): NEXT I
70   POKE  - 16300,0
80   FOR T = 1 TO (1200 / F)
90   NEXT T
100   POKE  - 16299,0
110   ONERR  GOTO 130
120   GOTO 70
130   TEXT : HOME : END
```

9

MOMENTUM

● ELASTIC COLLISION

When a billiard cue ball hits an object ball head on, they exchange momentum. Momentum is an object's mass times its velocity (speed in a certain direction). Try inputting different speeds for the two equal mass objects and observe what happens. What you see will only occur if objects are very elastic and don't stick together. Otherwise, the collision is called inelastic (*see* Car Crash at the end of this chapter).

Line 180 creates the sound.

Good shooting.

Program

```
10   REM   ELASTIC COLLISION
20   HOME : VTAB 23
30   GR : COLOR= 15: HLIN 0,39 AT
       39
40  X1 = 0:X2 = 39:Y = 38
50   INPUT "SPEED 1 (0-4)? ";V1
60   INPUT "SPEED 2 (0-4)? ";U
70  V2 =  - U
80  X1 = X1 + V1:X2 = X2 + V2
90   IF X1 >  = X2 THEN Q = V1:V1 =
      V2:V2 = Q: GOSUB 180
100   IF X1 > X2 THEN Q = X1:X1 =
      X2:X2 = Q
110   IF X1 < 0 OR X2 > 39 THEN 20
      0
120   COLOR= 9
130   PLOT X1,Y
140   COLOR= 2: PLOT X2,Y
150   FOR Z = 1 TO 500: NEXT Z
160   COLOR= 0: PLOT X1,Y: PLOT X2
      ,Y
170   GOTO 80
180 SO =  PEEK ( - 16336) +  PEEK
      ( - 16336)
190   RETURN
200   PRINT "AGAIN (Y/N)? ": GET A
      $
210   IF A$ = "Y" THEN 20
220   TEXT : HOME : END
```

● CANNON

The total momentum of a cannon and ball is the same before and after the gunpowder explosion. Momentum before the explosion is zero, since momentum equals mass times velocity and there is no velocity. After the explosion the mass × velocity of the cannonball is equal and opposite to the mass × velocity of the cannon. So the two momenta add up to zero.

Run the program. Observe the kickback of a light cannon compared to a heavy cannon. This program is very similar to the next program, Explosion.

Program

```
10   REM   CANNON
20   HOME : VTAB 24: HGR : HCOLOR=
     3
30  V1 = 10:C1 = 70:C2 = 71
40   PRINT "BALL MASS IS 1 KILOGRA
     M."
50   INPUT "CANNON MASS IN KILOGRA
     MS? ";KG
60   HGR
70   IF C1 < 10 OR C2 > 279 THEN   END

80   HPLOT 0,159 TO 279,159
90   HPLOT C2,157: HPLOT C1 + 10,1
     56 TO C1,156 TO C1,158 TO C1
      + 10,158
100  C2 = C2 + 10
110  C1 = C1 - 10 / KG
120   GOTO 60
```

● EXPLOSION

During an explosion, most of the solids and liquids in the explosive change to gases. The hot gases expand violently because they need more room than the original solids and liquids. Momentum is conserved during the explosion. This means that the sum of the mass times the speed of all the fragments going to the left equals the sum of the mass times the speed of all the fragments going to the right. The same goes for the up and down directions and front and back directions.

The firework in this program explodes into 15 fragments. Unlike a real explosion, the fragments move one at a time. This program flips between graphics pages one and two. While one is shown, the other is erased and redrawn.

Have a blast!

Program

```
10   REM   EXPLOSION
20   HOME : HGR : HGR2 : HCOLOR= 3

30 XX = 140:YY = 55: HPLOT XX,YY
40   DIM A(14,3)
50 N = 1
60   FOR Z = 0 TO 14
70 A(Z,0) = XX
80 A(Z,1) =   - 10 +   RND (1) * 20

90 A(Z,2) = YY
100 A(Z,3) =   - 10 +   RND (1) * 2
     0
110   NEXT Z
120   FOR T = 1 TO 15
130   POKE 230,32 * N: REM   DRAW O
     N PAGE N
140   FOR Z = 0 TO 14
150 A(Z,0) = A(Z,0) + A(Z,1)
160 X = A(Z,0)
170 A(Z,2) = A(Z,2) + A(Z,3)
180 Y = A(Z,2) + T ^ 2
190   IF X < 0 OR X > 279 OR Y < 0
     OR Y > 192 THEN 210
200   HPLOT X,Y
210   NEXT Z
220   IF N = 1 THEN   HGR2
230   IF N = 2 THEN   HGR : POKE   -
     16302,0
240   POKE   - 16301 + N,0: REM   DI
     SPLAY PAGE N
250 N =   ABS (3 - N)
260   NEXT T
270   TEXT : HOME
```

● CAR CRASH (INELASTIC COLLISION)

Picture two cars crashing and becoming one moving pileup. Or, picture a railroad car rolling into and coupling with a line of railroad cars. Both are examples of inelastic collisions. In equation form, (mass 1 × velocity 1) + (mass 2 × velocity 2) = mass 3 × velocity 3. Mass 3 is the combination of the two colliding masses.

Both cars in this program have the same mass. Compare the movement with that in the Elastic Collision program.

Drive carefully!

Program

```
10   REM   CAR CRASH (INELASTIC COL
      LISION)
20   HOME
30 X1 = 2:X2 = 38:Y = 38
40   GR : COLOR= 15: HLIN 0,39 AT
      39
50   INPUT "SPEED 1 (0 TO 5)? ";V1

60   INPUT "SPEED 2 (0 TO 5)? ";U
70 V2 =   - U
80 X1 = X1 + V1:X2 = X2 + V2
90   IF X1 >  = X2 THEN 150
100   COLOR= 1: PLOT X1,Y
110   COLOR= 13: PLOT X2,Y
120   FOR Z = 1 TO 500: NEXT Z
```

```
130    COLOR= 0: PLOT X1,Y: PLOT X2
       ,Y
140    GOTO 80
150 SO =    PEEK ( - 16336) +    PEEK
       ( - 16336)
160 X3 = (X1 + X2) / 2
170 V3 = (V1 + V2) / 2
180 X3 = X3 + V3
190    IF X3 < 0 OR X3 > 39 THEN 24
       0
200    COLOR= 9: PLOT X3,Y
210    FOR Z = 1 TO 500: NEXT Z
220    COLOR= 0: PLOT X3,Y
230    GOTO 180
240    PRINT "AGAIN (Y/N)?": GET A$

250    IF A$ = "Y" THEN 20
260    TEXT : HOME : END
```

10

MOTION IN A LINE

PROGRAMS

Constant Velocity
Acceleration
Deceleration
Gas-n-Brake
Drag Strip
Toss
Vertical Lander

● **CONSTANT VELOCITY**

Cruising at constant velocity means that there is no change in speed or direction. It is very important to understand this program because it is the basis for most Apple motion graphics. Let's cover this program line by line.

Line 10 clears the graphic screen. Line 20 keeps Y = 39. Y determines the number of characters down from the top of the screen that a character will be drawn.

Lines 40 through 90 form a loop in which X will increase from 0 to 39 by steps of one. The X position will go, therefore, from the left to right side of the screen. In Line 45 the color is made white. In Line 50 we plot the box on the screen. Line 60 is a nested time-delay loop which slows the action down while it counts to 100. In Lines 70 and 80 we change the box's color to the background black.

This painting, erasing, moving, painting, erasing, etc., creates movement or animation.

Program

```
5    REM    CONSTANT VELOCITY
10   GR
30 Y = 39
40   FOR X = 0 TO 39
45   COLOR= 15
50   PLOT X,Y
60   FOR Z = 1 TO 100: NEXT Z
70   COLOR= 0
80   PLOT X,Y
90   NEXT X
```

● ACCELERATION

A rocket accelerates when it is speeding up. When you step on the gas pedal of a car, the car accelerates. Acceleration is defined as rate of change in velocity. This program is different from constant velocity in that it is adding a number to the velocity in each loop. This number is called the acceleration. M/S/S is an abbreviation for acceleration in meters per second each second. The greater the acceleration, the faster the car or rocket speeds up. The Apple takes a picture of the car at equal time intervals.

90

Program

```
5   REM  ACCELERATION
10  X = 0:Y = 30:V = 0
20   HOME : GR
30   INPUT "ACCELERATION (0 TO 5 M
     ETERS/S/S)? ";A
40   FOR T = 1 TO 100
50   COLOR= 15
55   IF X > 39 THEN  END
60   PLOT X,Y
70   FOR Z = 0 TO 100: NEXT Z
100 V = V + A
110 X = X + V
120  NEXT T
```

● DECELERATION

Deceleration is a slowing down. A car decelerates when someone steps on the brake pedal. It is the same as a negative acceleration. The space shuttle *Columbia* decelerated when it reentered the earth's atmosphere because of air friction.

In Line 90 we subtract the deceleration (D) from the speed (S) of the car. This causes the slowing down.

Program

```
5   REM   DECELERATION
10   HOME : GR
20 X = 0
30   INPUT "SPEED (0 TO 10 METERS/
     S)? ";S
40   INPUT "DECELERATION (0 TO 10
     METERS/S/S)? ";D
50   FOR T = 1 TO 100
60   COLOR= 15
70   PLOT X,30
80   FOR Z = 1 TO 100: NEXT Z
90 S = S - D
100 X = X + S
110   IF S < = 0 OR X > = 39 THEN
        END
120   NEXT T
```

● GAS-N-BRAKE

Gas-n-Brake is a combination of the Acceleration and Deceleration programs. Line 70 reads the keyboard to see which, if any, key is depressed. P is equal to that character's ASCII* value. This allows us to change the motion on the screen without stopping the program from running. It is a very powerful line. It must be used with Line 80, which resets the memory location. When we put the → key, 1 is added to the velocity and the car accelerates. Pushing the ← key subtracts 1 from the velocity and slows down the car. The adding and subtracting are done in Line 90. If neither key is pressed, the car keeps going at constant velocity. Try using all four directions in the Docking program in Chapter 2.

*ASCII (pronounced *askey*) is the abbreviation for the American Standard Code for Information Interchange, which is now the code used in most microcomputers.

Program

```
10    REM   GAS-N-BRAKE
20    HOME
30  X = 0:Y = 38:V = 0
40    GR
50    COLOR= 15
60    HLIN 0,39 AT 39
70  P =   PEEK ( - 16384)
80    POKE  - 16368,0
90  V = V + (P = 149) - (P = 136)
100 X = X + V
110   IF X < 0 OR X > 39 THEN   END

120   COLOR= 3
130   PLOT X,Y
140   FOR T = 1 TO 500: NEXT T
150   GOTO 70
```

● **DRAG STRIP**

This is a fancy version of the Gas-n-Brake program. The idea is to get past the finish flag in the shortest time and then stop before hitting the wall. Press → to accelerate and press ← to brake. Your position each second is shown and the timer records which stage of the T-loop you are in.

Break some speed records, but don't break any walls.

Program

```
10   REM   DRAG STRIP
20   HOME :C = 0
30 X = 13:Y = 158:V = 1
40   HGR : HCOLOR= 3: HPLOT 0,159 TO
      279,159
50   HPLOT 275,158 TO 275,150 TO 2
      79,158
60   FOR XX = 220 TO 225
70   FOR YY = 146 TO 150
80   C =  ABS (1 - C)
90   IF C = 1 THEN  HPLOT XX,YY
```

```
100   NEXT YY
110   NEXT XX
120   FOR T = 1 TO 50
130   IF X > 220 THEN 150
140   HOME : VTAB 23: PRINT T;" SE
      CONDS"
150 KE =   PEEK ( - 16384): POKE  -
      16368,0: REM   READ KEYBOARD
160   IF KE = 149 THEN V = V + 1: REM
       GAS
170   IF KE = 136 THEN V = V - 1: REM
       BRAKE
180 X = X + V
190   IF X > 275 THEN   HCOLOR= 5: HPLOT
      272,Y TO 277,Y - 2 TO 275,Y -
      3 TO 272,Y: END
200   HCOLOR= 3: GOSUB 250
210   IF V = 0 THEN   TEXT : END
220   FOR Z = 1 TO 500: NEXT Z
230   HCOLOR= 0: GOSUB 250
240   NEXT T
250   HPLOT X,Y TO X,Y - 1 TO X -
      7,Y - 1 TO X - 7,Y - 2 TO X -
      8,Y - 2 TO X - 8,Y - 1 TO X -
      12,Y - 1 TO X - 12,Y TO X -
      11,Y TO X - 11,Y - 2
260   RETURN
```

● **TOSS**

The force of gravity pulls objects towards the earth. A ball tossed up in the air is always being pulled downward by this force. The force nicks away at the upward velocity given by the toss until the velocity is zero at the highest point of the toss. The gravitational force continues to work, causing the velocity to increase downward as the ball accelerates towards the ground.

Line 70 has the key equation for the height of the ball. The velocity of the toss times the elapsed time moves the ball upward while the acceleration due to gravity (T ↑ 2) pulls the ball downward.

Gravity wins!

Program

```
10   REM  TOSS
20   HOME : VTAB (24)
30   HGR : HCOLOR= 3
40   HPLOT 0,159 TO 279,159
50   INPUT "VELOCITY (0 TO 8 METER
     S/SECOND)? ";V
60   FOR T = 1 TO 50
70 Y = 159 - 3 * V * T + T ^ 2
80 X = 140
90   IF Y > 159 THEN   END
100   HCOLOR= 3
110   HPLOT X,Y TO X,Y - 1
120   FOR Z = 1 TO 100: NEXT Z
130   HCOLOR= 0
140   HPLOT X,Y TO X,Y - 1
150   NEXT T
```

● VERTICAL LANDER

Soft land a spacecraft on the moon before fuel runs out. All you have to do is use your thruster engine cautiously. Keep an eye on your instrument panel. A negative velocity indicates that you are moving downward. A downward velocity faster than –3 m/s when landing means a crash. Your altitude is given in meters (m).

Challenge a friend to (a) safely land and conserve more fuel than you did or (b) safely land in less time than you can.

Want to get the feel of landing the spacecraft on earth? In Lines 190 and 200 change the 1 to 5. This is necessary because the acceleration due to gravity is more than five times greater on earth.

Program

```
10    TEXT
20    REM  VERTICAL LANDER
30    HOME : VTAB 24
40    HGR : HCOLOR= 3: HPLOT 0,159 TO
      279,159
50 X = 140
60 FU = 100
70 T = 0
80 HT = 400
90 VE =   - 30
100 L = 158 - HT / 3
110   IF L < 0 THEN 140
120   HCOLOR= 3: GOSUB 320
130   IF HT <  = 0 AND VE <  =  -
      3 THEN 300
140   IF HT <  = 0 AND VE >  - 3 THEN
      310
150   INPUT "THRUST (0 TO 20)? ";T
      H
160   IF FU < TH THEN 150
170   IF TH > 20 THEN 150
180   HCOLOR= 0: GOSUB 320
190 HT = HT + VE - 1 + TH
200 VE = VE - 1 + TH
210 FU = FU - TH
220 T = T + 1
230   HOME : VTAB 24
240   PRINT T;" S";
250   IF HT < 0 THEN HT = 0
260   PRINT  SPC( 7) INT (HT);" M"

270   PRINT FU;" FUEL UNITS"
280   PRINT VE;" M/S"
290   GOTO 100
300   INVERSE : PRINT "CRASH LANDI
      NG": NORMAL : END
310   INVERSE : PRINT "SAFE LANDIN
      G": NORMAL : END
```

```
320   HPLOT X,L TO X - 5,L - 6 TO
      X + 5,L - 6 TO X,L
330   HPLOT X - 5,L - 6 TO X - 10,
      L
340   HPLOT X + 5,L - 6 TO X + 10,
      L
350   RETURN
```

11

MOTION IN TWO DIMENSIONS

● HORIZONTAL THROW

Throw a ball parallel to the ground and plot its movement. Does it stay in the air any longer if it is thrown faster? How about when it is just dropped?

Motion in two dimensions needs different equations for the X and Y directions. Line 80 gives the X position which is related to velocity times time. There is no air friction taken into account. Line 90 gives the Y position, which is accelerating downward. Does the X position affect the Y position?

104

Program

```
10   REM   HORIZONTAL THROW
20   HOME : VTAB (24)
30   HGR : HCOLOR= 3
40   HPLOT 0,159 TO 279,159
50   INPUT "VELOCITY (0 TO 45 M/S)
     ? ";V
60   FOR T = 0 TO 9
70   FOR Z = 1 TO 300: NEXT Z
80 X = 2 * V * T
90 Y = 82 - T ^ 2
100  IF X > 279 OR Y < 0 THEN  END

110  HPLOT X,159 - Y
120  NEXT T
```

● **MARBLE ROLLS OFF TABLE**

This is a jazzed-up version of the Horizontal Throw program. The tricky part of this program is to keep the marble from dropping until it reaches the end of the table. The conditional Lines 110 and 120 take care of this.

Program

```
10   REM  MARBLE ROLLS OFF TABLE
20   HOME : VTAB 24
30   HGR : HCOLOR= 3
40   HPLOT 0,30 TO 30,30
50   HPLOT 15,30 TO 15,150
60   HPLOT 0,151 TO 279,151
70   INPUT "VELOCITY (1 TO 50)? ";
     V
80 Y = 29:X = 0
90  FOR T = 0 TO 50
100 X = V * T
110  IF X <  = 29 THEN  GOSUB 190

120  IF X > 29 THEN T2 = T2 + 1
130  FOR Z = 1 TO 300: NEXT Z
140 Y = T2 ^ 2 + 29
150  IF X > 279 THEN  END
160  IF Y > 151 THEN  END
170  HPLOT X,Y
180  NEXT T
190 T2 = 0
200  RETURN
```

● TRAJECTORY

Fire a cannon and hit the target. The path of the cannonball is called its trajectory. You have to decide on the angle of elevation of the cannon, which is the angle between the ground and the gun. You also must judge what powder charge is needed.

Is there only one elevation angle that will cause the cannonball to land on one spot using the same charge? Try 30 degrees and 60 degrees.

Which angle of elevation fires the ball farthest from the cannon? Try it. This program doesn't take air friction into account. If there was air friction, would you increase or decrease the angle of elevation to shoot the cannonball the farthest downfield?

Program

```
10   REM   TRAJECTORY
20   HOME
30   VTAB (24)
40 Z = 20 +  RND (1) * 244
50   HGR : HCOLOR= 3
60   HPLOT 0,159 TO 279,159
70   HPLOT 0,159 TO 7,152
80   HPLOT Z,158 TO Z,148 TO Z + 1
     5,148 TO Z + 15,158 TO Z,158

90   INPUT "DEGREES ELEVATION (0 T
     O 90)? ";DE
100   INPUT "CHARGE (0 TO 4)? ";C
110 U = 7 *  SIN (DE / 180 * 3.14
     )
120 R = 7 *  COS (DE / 180 * 3.14
     )
130   HCOLOR= 0
140   HPLOT 0,159 TO 7,152
150   HCOLOR= 3
160   HPLOT 0,159 TO R,159 - U
170   FOR T = 1 TO 50
180 Y = U * C * T - T ^ 2
190 X = R * C * T
200   IF Y > 159 THEN 230
210   IF Y < 1 OR X > 279 THEN  END

220   HPLOT X,159 - Y
230   NEXT T
```

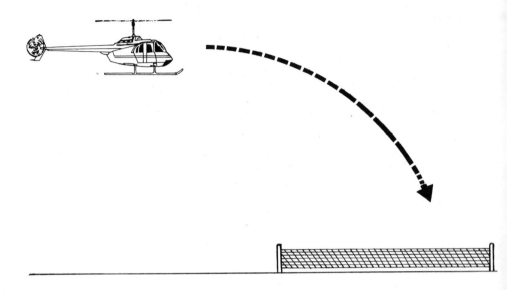

● HELICOPTER

Take the controls of a helicopter and land the helicopter safely in the enclosure. Come in too fast and no more helicopter. Press ↑ for up, ← for left, and → for right.

Air drag is built into this program in Line 140. Five percent of the horizontal velocity here is lost in each time interval.

Land carefully.

Program

```
10   REM   HELICOPTER
20   HGR2 : HCOLOR= 3
30   HPLOT 0,191 TO 279,191
40   HPLOT 230,190 TO 230,183
50   HPLOT 250,190 TO 250,183
60 X = 30:Y = 30
70 VX = 0:VY = 0
80   FOR T = 0 TO 100
```

```
90  VY = VY + .5
100 KE =  PEEK ( - 16384): POKE  -
    16368,0
110  IF KE = 139 THEN VY = VY - 1
    .5: REM  UP KEY
120  IF KE = 149 THEN VX = VX + 1
    .1: REM  RIGHT KEY
130  IF KE = 136 THEN VX = VX - 1
    .1: REM  LEFT KEY
140 X = X + .95 * VX
150 Y = Y + VY
160  IF Y = 189 AND VY < 2 THEN 1
    67
163  GOTO 170
167  HCOLOR= 3: HPLOT X + 1,Y + 1
    TO X - 3,Y + 1: HPLOT X - 3
    ,Y TO X + 3,Y: END
170  IF Y < 2 OR X < 5 OR X > 274
    THEN  END
180  HCOLOR= 3: HPLOT X + 1,Y + 1
    TO X - 3,Y + 1
190  FOR RE = 1 TO 30
200  HCOLOR= 3: HPLOT X - 3,Y TO
    X,Y
210 SO =  PEEK ( - 16336)
220  HCOLOR= 0: HPLOT X - 3,Y TO
    X,Y
230  HCOLOR= 3: HPLOT X + 3,Y TO
    X,Y
240 SO =  PEEK ( - 16336)
250  HCOLOR= 0: HPLOT X + 3,Y TO
    X,Y
260  NEXT RE
270  HCOLOR= 0: HPLOT X + 1,Y + 1
    TO X - 3,Y + 1
280  NEXT T
```

● RIVER CROSSING

You are a boat captain taking your ferry to the other side of the river. The river is flowing from left to right on your screen. The ferry starts at the bottom center of the screen and the home pier is at the top center of the screen. Right (downriver) is 0 degrees, straight across is 90 degrees, and left (upriver) is 180 degrees.

The ferry will point in the direction you input. If the river is flowing at 0 miles per hour, the angle that you input is the direction the ferry will travel. If the river is flowing, however, the ferry won't travel in the direction it is pointing. Your job is to point the ferry in the correct direction to get it to the pier. This is called choosing the correct heading. Where you wind up also depends on the ferry speed.

All ashore that's going ashore!

Program

```
10   REM   RIVER CROSSING
20   HOME
30 X = 140:Y = 1
40   HGR
50   VTAB (24)
60   HCOLOR= 3
70   HPLOT 0,0 TO 279,0
80   HPLOT 0,159 TO 279,159
90   HPLOT 138,0 TO 138,8 TO 142,8
        TO 142,0
100   HPLOT 140,158
110   HPLOT 0,80 TO 15,80 TO 10,75
        TO 15,80 TO 10,85
120   INPUT "RIVER FLOW (0 TO 5 MP
      H)? ";R
130   INPUT "BOAT SPEED (0 TO 10 M
      PH)? ";B
140   PRINT "RIGHT IS 0 DEGREES;LE
      FT IS 180 DEGREES."
150   INPUT "BOAT HEADING (0 TO 18
      0 DEGREES)? ";D
160 BX = B *  COS (D / 180 * 3.14
      )
170 BY = B *  SIN (D / 180 * 3.14
      )
180 X = X + BX + R
190 Y = Y + BY
200   IF X < 0 OR X > 279 OR Y < 0
        OR Y > 159 THEN  END
210   HPLOT X,159 - Y
220   GOTO 160
```

● PENDULUM

The simplest pendulum is made up of a small weight (bob) hanging from a string. The period of vibration is the time it takes a pendulum to swing back and forth once. The Italian scientist Galileo discovered that each pendulum has a constant period no matter how far it swings back and forth. Clocks make use of this principle.

The sine and cosine functions drive the movement of the swing shown on the Apple. The value of sine goes from zero to one to zero to one, etc. Sine value determines the height of the swing seat and cosine determines its side-to-side motion. Together they make it behave like a pendulum.

Have a swinging time!

Program

```
10   REM   PENDULUM
20   HOME
30 L = 130:XX = 140:YY = 3
40 S = 8
50   FOR A = 0 TO 50 * 3.14 STEP 3
     .14 / 16
60   HGR2 : HCOLOR= 3
70 X = XX +   COS (A) * L
80 Y = YY +   ABS ( SIN (A) * L)
90   HPLOT X + S,Y TO X - S,Y TO X
     ,Y TO XX,YY
100   NEXT A
110   TEXT
```

What is wrong with this picture?

● SAILBOAT RACE

This program gives you the feel of a sailboat with all the frustra-
tions of not always being able to sail in the direction that you wish to
go. Sailboats can go with the wind at their backs and also with the
wind at their sides. They cannot sail directly into the wind. The best a
sailboat can do is point 30 degrees off the direction from which the
wind is blowing.

Draw for yourself a compass rose and keep it by your computer. It

116

will be helpful during the race. On an index card or piece of paper draw a circle. Write 360 degrees at the top of the circle, 90 degrees at the right side, 180 degrees at the bottom, and 270 degrees at the left side. 360 degrees represents north, which is at the top of your screen.

The first input you are asked for is "WIND FROM?" Choose any direction you like. For instance, 45 degrees means that the wind is coming from the upper-right part of the screen. The second requested input is "HEADING?" This is the direction you wish to sail. Once the Apple has this information it will start tracking your position on the screen. If the boat reaches the sides or top or bottom of the screen, the race is over. So you need to change your course before crashing into the top or bottom or the island. Do this any time by pressing any key. The Apple will then ask for a new heading.

Challenge a friend to a race around the island, and back across the starting line. The boat completing the course in the shortest time wins.

Program

```
5   TEXT : HOME
10   PRINT  TAB( 15)"SAILBOAT RACE
     "
20   VTAB (8)
30   PRINT "SAIL YOUR BOAT (.) ACR
     OSS THE SCREEN"
40   PRINT "OR AROUND THE ISLAND A
     ND BACK. NORTH "
50   PRINT "(360 DEGREES) IS TOWAR
     DS THE TOP OF THE"
60   PRINT "SCREEN. SHOW DIRECTION
     S IN DEGREES (0 "
70   PRINT "TO 360). PRESS ANY KEY
     TO CHANGE "
80   PRINT "HEADING.": PRINT
90   PRINT "PRESS ANY KEY."
100 P =  PEEK ( - 16384): POKE  -
     16368,0
110  IF P <  = 127 THEN  GOTO 100
```

```
120   HOME
130   VTAB 22
140   HGR : HCOLOR= 3: HPLOT 1,79
150   FOR A = 0 TO 6.28 STEP .1
160 X = 200 + 8 *  COS (A):Y = 80
        + 8 *  SIN (A)
170   HPLOT X,Y: NEXT A
180 X = 1:Y = 80: HPLOT 135,10 TO
        135,5 TO 139,10 TO 139,5
190   HPLOT 0,20 TO 0,0 TO 279,0 TO
        279,159 TO 0,159 TO 0,139
200   INPUT "WIND FROM? ";WI
210   FOR T = 1 TO 300
220   IF T > 1 THEN 240
230   INPUT "HEADING? ";HE
240 P =  PEEK ( - 16384): POKE  -
        16368,0
250   IF P >  = 127 THEN  GOTO 230

260 R =  ABS (HE - WI)
270   IF R > 180 THEN R = 360 - R
280   IF R <  = 90 THEN V = .15 *
        R - 3.5
290   IF R > 90 THEN V = 10 - (R -
        90) * .04
300 X = X + (V *  COS (((360 - HE
        ) + 90) / 180 * 3.14))
310 Y = Y + (V *  SIN (((360 - HE
        ) + 90) / 180 * 3.14))
320   IF X <  = 0 OR X >  = 279 OR
        Y <  = 0 OR Y >  = 159 THEN
        END
330   HOME : VTAB (22): PRINT "HOU
        R ";T
340   HPLOT X,159 - Y
350   FOR Z = 1 TO 100: NEXT Z
360   NEXT T
```

12

POSITION, MAPPING, AND DESIGN

PROGRAMS

Radio Direction Finder
Radar
Sonar
Hi-Resolution 3-D Drawing
Topographic Map

● RADIO DIRECTION FINDER

A radio direction finder enables airplanes and ships to find their location. It is merely a radio antenna on a pivot which is turned in the direction that the radio volume is loudest. The direction of the transmitting radio station can then be determined with a compass. Signals from two or more radio stations are needed to find the geographical location of a plane or ship.

The Apple draws on the screen a map showing the position of Radio Station 1 and Radio Station 2. North direction (0 degrees or 360 degrees) is toward the top of the screen. Your ship is at sea someplace in the area of the map. The radio direction finder on your ship gives you the compass headings for the two radio stations. You need to figure out where you are.

You'll need the following materials:

1. a small, circular protractor with 360 degrees

2. a felt-tip pen with highlight washable ink

3. a ruler, preferably plastic

4. a paper towel

Follow these directions:

1. Hold the protractor with 0 degrees or 360 degrees facing upward on the TV screen.

2. Read the compass heading for Radio Station 1.

3. Using your other hand or a friend's hand, place the edge of the ruler over the protractor so that it touches the center of the protractor and the correct compass heading.

4. Slide the protractor and ruler together so that the edge of the ruler touches Radio Station 1. Always be sure to have 0 degrees facing upward and the ruler keeping the correct heading.

5. Draw a line on the TV screen along the ruler's edge.

6. Repeat directions 1 through 5 for Radio Station 2.

The place where the two lines cross is your boat's location. Press any key to see how close you came to your real position. Clean the screen with the paper towel when you are finished.

Program

```
10   REM   RADIO DIRECTION FINDER
20   HOME : VTAB 24
30   HGR : HCOLOR= 3
40 A = 5 +   RND (1) * 270
50 B = 10 +   RND (1) * 140
60   HPLOT 0,3 TO 3,0 TO 3,7
70   HPLOT 275,0 TO 279,0 TO 279,3
        TO 275,3 TO 275,6 TO 279,6
80   HPLOT 138,7 TO 138,0 TO 142,7
        TO 142,0
90 X = A:Y = 159 - B
100 LE =   INT (270.5 + ( ATN (Y /
        X)) * 180 / 3.14)
110 R = 279 - A
120 RI =   INT (90.5 - ( ATN (Y /
        R)) * 180 / 3.14)
130   PRINT LE;" DEGREES TO 1
        ";RI;" DEGREES TO 2"
140   INVERSE
150   PRINT "PRESS ANY KEY FOR POS
        ITION.": NORMAL
160   GET C$
170 BB = 159 - B
180   HPLOT A - 3,BB + 3 TO A + 3,
        BB - 3
190   HPLOT A + 3,BB + 3 TO A - 3,
        BB - 3
```

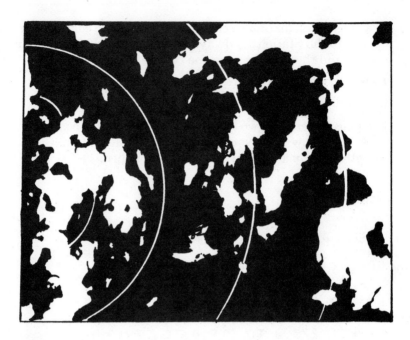

● RADAR

The TV monitor acts like a radar screen when the Apple runs this program. Radar is an electronic instrument which can detect objects by sending radio waves to them and receiving radio waves reflected from them. Radar can show us the direction and distance of objects.

On your ship's radar screen your vessel is always in the center of the picture. The front of your boat always faces the top of the screen. Key [↑] to move the ship forward, [←] to turn toward the left, and [→] to turn toward the right. The further away islands are from you on the screen, the further away they would really be.

Program

```
10   REM  RADAR
20  XX = 140:YY = 95
30  T = 0: DIM I(9,1)
40   FOR Z = 0 TO 9
50  R =   RND (1) * 80
```

```
60 A = (3 * 3.14 / 2) + (2 * 3.14
      / 9) * Z
70 I(Z,0) = R *  COS (A)
80 I(Z,1) = R *  SIN (A)
90   NEXT Z
100   HGR2
110 T = T + 1
120 KE =  PEEK ( - 16384): POKE  -
      16368,0
130   IF KE = 149 THEN AN =  - 10 /
      180 * 3.14: REM   RIGHT TURN
140   IF KE = 136 THEN AN = 10 / 1
      80 * 3.14: REM   LEFT TURN
150   IF KE < 127 OR KE = 139 THEN
      AN = 0
160   FOR Z = 0 TO 9
170 X =  COS (2 * 3.14 * Z / 9) *
      90 + XX
180 Y =  SIN (2 * 3.14 * Z / 9) *
      90 + YY
190   HCOLOR= 3
200   HPLOT XX,YY TO X,Y
210   HCOLOR= 0
220   HPLOT XX,YY TO X,Y
230   HCOLOR= 3
240   IF KE = 139 THEN I(Z,1) = I(
      Z,1) + 2: REM   MOVE FORWARD
250 Q = I(Z,0)
260 I(Z,0) = I(Z,0) *  COS (AN) -
      I(Z,1) *  SIN (AN)
270 I(Z,1) = Q *  SIN (AN) + I(Z,
      1) *  COS (AN)
280   IF I(Z,0) <  - 90 OR I(Z,0) >
      90 OR I(Z,1) <  - 90 OR I(Z,
      1) > 90 THEN 300
290   HPLOT I(Z,0) + XX,I(Z,1) + Y
      Y TO I(Z,0) + XX,I(Z,1) + YY
      + 1
300   NEXT Z
310   GOTO 100
```

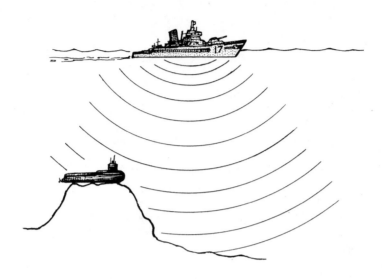

● SONAR

This program is a game. The object is to find a submarine which is stuck on the sea bottom and save its crew before they run out of air. You are a ship sonar operator. Instruct your captain on the direction he or she should steer to find the sub in distress. Do this by pressing arrow keys. Watch your screen for the position of your ship and for the remaining time. The screen gives an aerial view.

But how do you know which direction to tell the captain to go? Well, sonar is an instrument which uses sound to locate underwater objects. The sound is sent out from your ship, reflects off the grounded sub, and is heard by you on the sonar. The closer you are to the sub in distress, the closer together the sounds come.

With practice you should be able to do this with your eyes closed.

Program

```
10   REM   SONAR
20   HOME
30   X = 140:Y = 80:T = 100
40   XX =   RND (1) * 239
50   YY =   RND (1) * 159
```

```
60  KE =  PEEK ( - 16384): POKE  -
    16368,0
70  IF X > 270 THEN 90
80  IF KE = 149 THEN X = X + 3
90  IF X < 3 THEN 110
100  IF KE = 136 THEN X = X - 3
110  IF Y < 3 THEN 130
120  IF KE = 139 THEN Y = Y - 3
130  IF Y > 156 THEN 150
140  IF KE = 138 THEN Y = Y + 3
150  HGR : HCOLOR= 3
160  HPLOT X,Y
170  IF KE > 127 THEN NE = KE
180  IF NE = 149 OR NE = 136 THEN
     HPLOT X + 2,Y TO X - 2,Y
190  IF NE = 139 OR NE = 138 THEN
     HPLOT X,Y + 2 TO X,Y - 2
200 D = ((XX - X) ^ 2 + (YY - Y) ^
    2) ^ .5
210  GOSUB 320
220  FOR TI = 1 TO D * 5: NEXT TI

230  GOSUB 320
240 T = T - 1
250  IF T = 0 THEN  PRINT "TOO LA
    TE.": END
260  HOME : VTAB 21
270  PRINT  INT (10 * D);" YARDS"

280  PRINT T;" HOURS LEFT"
290  IF X < XX + 2 AND X > XX - 2
     AND Y < YY + 2 AND Y > YY -
    2 THEN  PRINT "SAVED. GOOD S
    HOW!": TEXT : END
300  FOR Z = 1 TO 100: NEXT Z
310  GOTO 60
320 SO =  PEEK ( - 16336) -  PEEK
    ( - 16336)
330  RETURN
```

● HI-RESOLUTION 3-D DRAWING

The authors have to boast that this program is truly amazing. It shows the real power that computers possess.

Enter the program as is. Then run it. Input 0 degrees clockwise, 0 degrees upright, and size = 1. The Apple will then draw a front view of a box. Run the program again with 30 degrees clockwise and 30 degrees upright. *Voila!* Right before your eyes is the same box seen from another perspective. Try some more views. If the program bombs, make the box a smaller size, such as an .8, so that it doesn't go off the screen.

Ready to draw your own picture? Your data is entered as X, Y, Z coordinates for the first point; X, Y, Z for the second point; etc. Make your last data 999,999,999 to signal the Apple that there is no more data. The absolute value of the X, Y, and Z coordinates can't exceed 50. Negative Z values come out of the screen. The program is set up to draw lines between points 1 and 2, 2 and 3, 3 and 4, etc. You will have to put the coordinates in the proper order.

The loop from Lines 140 to 220 acts as a slave and moves the points on your picture one by one to draw the picture from the new perspective.

Program

```
10   REM   HI-RESOLUTION 3-D

20   HOME :Z =  - 1: VTAB (23)
```

```
30    INPUT "DEGREES CLOCKWISE? ";A

40    INPUT "DEGREES UPRIGHT? ";AA
50    INPUT "SIZE (0 TO 1)? ";S
60    DIM I(60,2)
70 Z = Z + 1
80    READ I(Z,0),I(Z,1),I(Z,2)
90    IF I(Z,0) = 999 THEN 110
100    GOTO 70
110    HGR : HCOLOR= 3
120 A = A * 3.14 / 180
130 AA = AA * 3.14 / 180
140    FOR C = 0 TO Z
150 QX = I(C,0)
160 I(C,0) = I(C,0) *  COS (A) -
      I(C,1) *  SIN (A)
170 QY = I(C,1)
180 I(C,1) = QX *  SIN (A) + I(C,
      1) *  COS (A)
190 QZ = I(C,2)
200 I(C,2) = I(C,2) *  COS (AA) -
      I(C,1) *  SIN (AA)
210 I(C,1) = QZ *  SIN (AA) + I(C
      ,1) *  COS (AA)
220    NEXT C
230    FOR C = 0 TO Z - 2
240    HPLOT 140 + S * I(C,0),80 +
      S * I(C,1) TO 140 + S * I(C +
      1,0),80 + S * I(C + 1,1)
250    NEXT C
260    DATA  -50,-50,-50,50,-50,-50
      ,50,50,-50,-50,50,-50,-50,-5
      0,-50,-50,-50,50,-50,50,50,5
      0,50,50,50,50,-50,50,-50,-50

270    DATA  50,-50,50,-50,-50,50,-
      50,50,50,-50,50,-50,50,50,-5
      0,50,50,50,50,-50,50
280    DATA  999,999,999
```

● TOPOGRAPHIC MAP

This program instructs the Apple to make a smooth topographic map on the screen. A topographic map shows the position and elevation of things such as mountains and valleys. The lowest areas will be COLOR = 0 (black). As altitude increases, color changes—COLOR = 1 (magenta) up to COLOR = 9 (orange).

When running the program, input the lowest (minimum) elevation and the highest (maximum) elevation that will be on the map. Then move the blinking cursor with the arrow keys to any place on the map where the elevation is known. Press [I] and input the elevation. Repeat the process for all the locations where you know the elevation. Then press [D] and the Apple will draw the topographic map. It takes a while, but it is fun to watch.

You can use the program for other things too, such as bathymetric (underwater) maps, pictures of animals and plants, or even for maps of numbers of an insect found in different places in your backyard.

Program

```
10   TEXT : HOME
20   VTAB (7): PRINT  TAB( 10)"COL
     OR TOPOGRAPHIC MAP"
30   VTAB (12)
40   PRINT "KEY ARROWS TO MOVE CUR
     SOR.
50   PRINT "KEY I TO INPUT VALUE."
60   PRINT "KEY D TO DRAW."
70   PRINT : PRINT : PRINT "PRESS
     ANY KEY."
80   P =  PEEK ( - 16384): POKE  -
     16368,0
90   IF P < = 127 THEN 80
100  HOME
110  VTAB (10): INPUT "MINIMUM VA
     LUE? ";MI
120  INPUT "MAXIMUM VALUE? ";MA
130  HOME
140  DIM V(300,2)
150  R3 = 0:XX = 1:V = 0:X = 20:Y =
     20
160  GR : COLOR= 15
170  PLOT X,Y
180  P =  PEEK ( - 16384): POKE  -
     16368,0
190  IF P > 127 THEN  HOME
200  IF X = 39 THEN 220
210  IF P = 149 THEN X = X + 1: REM
     MOVES CURSOR RIGHT
220  IF X = 0 THEN 240
230  IF P = 136 THEN X = X - 1: REM
     MOVES CURSOR LEFT
240  IF Y = 39 THEN 260
250  IF P = 138 THEN Y = Y + 1: REM
     MOVES CURSOR DOWN
260  IF Y = 0 THEN 280
```

```
270   IF P = 139 THEN Y = Y - 1: REM
         MOVES CURSOR UP
280   PLOT X,Y
290   IF P = 201 THEN 320: REM   IN
         PUT DECISION
300   IF P = 196 THEN 390: REM   DR
         AW DECISION
310   GOTO 160
320   HOME
330   VTAB (24): INPUT "VALUE? ";V
         (XX,2)
340 V(XX,0) = Y
350 V(XX,1) = X
360 XX = XX + 1
370 Z = XX
380   GOTO 160
390   FOR X = 0 TO 39
400   FOR Y = 0 TO 39
410   FOR XX = 1 TO Z
420 R2 = (Y - V(XX,0)) ^ 2 + (X -
         V(XX,1)) ^ 2
430   IF R2 = 0 THEN R2 = .001
440 V = V + (V(XX,2) / R2)
450 R3 = R3 + (1 / R2)
460   NEXT XX
470 VA = V / R3
480 U = (MA - MI) / 10
490   FOR B = 9 TO 0 STEP  - 1
500   IF VA <  = U * (B + 1) + MI THEN
         COLOR= B: PLOT X,Y
510   NEXT B
520 V = 0:R3 = 0
530   NEXT Y
540   NEXT X
```

13

PSYCHOLOGY

PROGRAMS

Memory Test
Reaction Time

● MEMORY TEST

Our minds keep a record of our earlier experiences. This mental record is called memory. Psychologists, scientists who study the mind, tell us that memory loss is greatest shortly after we learn something. After that we forget more slowly.

This test has simple guidelines. Run the program. As soon as the letters appear on the screen, work your hardest to memorize them in order. After one minute they will disappear. Then enter the letters in the order in which you remember them, keying [RETURN] after each one. Guess if you are not sure. After you input 15 letters, the Apple will tell you the number you got correct, as well as show you the computer letters next to your letters.

Compare your scores answering the test right away and answering another test 15 minutes after seeing the letters.

Program

```
10   REM   MEMORY TEST
20 N = 0
30   HOME
40   VTAB (10)
50   DIM A$(14,1)
60   FOR I = 0 TO 14
70 A$ =   CHR$ ( RND (1) * 25 + 65
     )
80 A$(I,0) = A$: PRINT A$;" ";
90   NEXT I
100   VTAB (20)
110   PRINT : PRINT : PRINT "YOU H
      AVE ONE MINUTE."
120   FOR Z = 1 TO 42000: NEXT Z
130   FOR Z = 1 TO 10
140 SO =   PEEK ( - 16336)
150   NEXT Z
160   HOME
170   PRINT "ENTER THE LETTERS IN
      ORDER.
180   PRINT "KEY [RETURN] AFTER EA
      CH LETTER.
190   PRINT "GUESS IF YOU ARE NOT
      SURE.
200   PRINT
210   FOR I = 0 TO 14
220   INPUT A$
230 A$(I,1) = A$
240   IF A$(I,0) = A$(I,1) THEN N =
      N + 1
250   NEXT I
260   HOME
270   FOR I = 0 TO 14
280   PRINT A$(I,0);" ";A$(I,1)
290   NEXT I
300   PRINT : PRINT N;" CORRECT"
```

● REACTION TIME

A change in the environment that causes us to respond is called a stimulus. A stimulus can be a sight, sound, smell, taste, or touch. Often a response to a stimulus is a movement. The time between the stimulus and the response is the reaction time.

Test your reaction time by running this program. After a random period of time the word FLASH will appear on the screen. Hit any key as soon as you see it. The Apple will then give your reaction time in hundredths of a second.

It is pretty impressive, isn't it? Your reaction time, that is. Especially is you take into consideration that a nerve impulse had to go from your eye to your brain to the flexor muscles in your fingers in that time. Also, you had to move your finger.

Program

```
10   REM   REACTION TIME
20   HOME : VTAB (10)
30   FOR I = 1 TO 1000 +   RND (1) *
     10000
40   NEXT I
50   INVERSE
60   PRINT "**FLASH**********FLASH
     **********FLASH**"
70   FOR T = 1 TO 10000
80   X =   PEEK ( - 16384): POKE   -
     16368,0
90   IF X > 127 THEN 110
100   NEXT T
110   PRINT : PRINT   INT (100 * T /
      47.5);" HUNDRETHS OF A SECON
      D"
120   NORMAL
```

14

WAVES (SOUND, LIGHT, AND WATER)

PROGRAMS

Lightning and Thunder
Amplitude and Wavelength
Reflection

● LIGHTNING AND THUNDER

Lightning is a huge electrical spark that lights up the night sky. It heats up the air, causing the air to expand like an explosion and create the sound of thunder. The sound of thunder reaches us after we see the lightning. The light travels almost instantaneously at 186,280 miles (299,790 kilometers) per second. Sound travels at only 1100 feet (335 meters) per second. If you count the seconds between seeing lightning and hearing thunder, you can estimate how far away the lightning is. Sound travels one mile in about five seconds.

In this program you input how far away the storm is. Pretend you are looking out your window instead of watching the TV monitor.

138

Program

```
10   REM  LIGHTNING AND THUNDER
20   HOME
30   INPUT "DISTANCE IN MILES? ";D

40 T = D / (1087 / 5280)
50   HGR2 : HCOLOR= 3
60   FOR Z = 1 TO 3000: NEXT Z
70   HPLOT 100,0 TO 150,191
80  .HGR2
90   FOR TI = 1 TO 1200 * T
100   NEXT TI
110   FOR Z = 1 TO 10:SO =   PEEK (
      - 16336): NEXT Z
120   TEXT : HOME
```

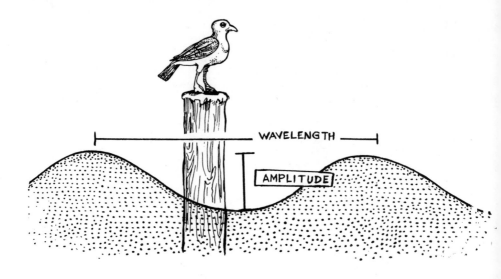

● AMPLITUDE AND WAVELENGTH

The amplitude of a wave is the distance it is disturbed from the resting stage. For a water wave, the amplitude is the height of the wave above calm water level. The amplitude of a wave is a measure of its energy. The high points of waves are called crests and the low points are called troughs. Wavelength is the distance between wave crests.

Wavelengths vary a whole lot. A tsunami can have a wavelength 1000 kilometers long. Some radio waves have 1000-meter wavelengths. Gamma rays and X-rays, both of which are waves, have wavelengths smaller than 10^{-10} (or .0000000001) meters.

Make your own waves on the TV monitor by inputting different amplitudes and wavelengths.

Program

```
10  REM  AMPLITUDE AND WAVELENGTH

20    HOME
30    VTAB 24
40    HGR
50    HCOLOR= 3
60    INPUT "WAVELENGTH (0 TO 300)?
         ";W
70    INPUT "AMPLITUDE (0 TO 75)? "
      ;A
80   FOR I = 0 TO 100 STEP .1
90  X = I * W / 6.28
100 Y = 80 + A *  SIN (I)
110   IF X > 279 THEN   END
120   IF Y < 0 OR Y > 159 THEN   GOTO
      140
130   HPLOT X,Y
140   NEXT I
```

● REFLECTION

Reflection is the return of wave energy, such as sound, radio, or light after it strikes a surface. It is similar to the action of a ball rebounding off a wall. An angle formed by the path of the thrown ball and a line perpendicular to the wall at the point of contact is the angle of incidence. The corresponding angle made by the rebounding ball is the angle of reflection. The two angles should always be equal.

Sound waves reflect as echoes. Sonar instruments make use of this principle. We see reflected light in a mirror. Radar makes use of reflected radio waves.

Watch the wave energy reflect off the edges. Notice how the absolute speed in the X and Y direction never changes.

142

Program

```
10   REM   REFLECTION
20   HOME : VTAB (10)
30   INPUT "INCIDENT ANGLE (0 TO 9
     0 DEGREES)? ";A
40 X = 3:Y = 96
50   HGR2 : HCOLOR= 3
60   HPLOT 0,0 TO 279,0 TO 279,191
     TO 0,191 TO 0,0
70 VX = 2 *  COS ((A - 90) / 180 *
     3.14)
80 VY = 2 *  SIN ((A - 90) / 180 *
     3.14)
90   IF Y >  = 189 OR Y <  = 2 THEN
     VY =  - VY
100   IF X >  = 277 OR X <  = 2 THEN
     VX =  - VX
110 X = X + VX:Y = Y + VY
120   HPLOT X,Y
130   GOTO 90
```

index

DATE DUE